conn

BIBLE STUDY GUIDE
LARGE PRINT EDITION

Correction &
Counsel

A STUDY OF
1 & 2 Corinthians

Sharon Gritz

Tom Howe

Ed Jordan

Julie Wood

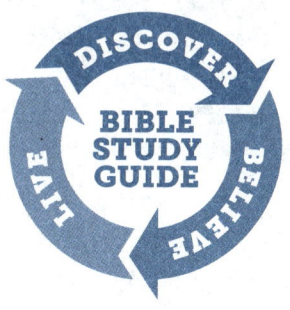

DISCOVER

BIBLE
STUDY
GUIDE

BELIEVE

LIVE

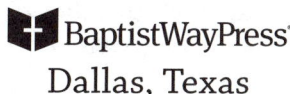

BaptistWayPress®
Dallas, Texas

Correction and Counsel (A Study of 1 & 2 Corinthians)—
Connect 360 Bible Study Guide—Large Print Edition

BAPTISTWAY PRESS® Leadership Team
Executive Director, Baptist General Convention of Texas: David Hardage
Associate Executive Director, Baptist General Convention of Texas: Steve Vernon
Director, Great Commission Team: Delvin Atchison
Publisher, BaptistWay Press®: Bob Billups
Publishing Consultant: Scott Stevens
Marketing Coordinator: Stan Granberry

Cover: Micah Kandros Design
Interior Design and Production: Desktop Miracles, Inc.
Printing: Data Reproductions Corporation

First edition: September 2018
ISBN–13978–1–938355–95–0

How to Make the Best Use of This Issue

Whether you're the teacher or a student—

1. Start early in the week before your class meets.

2. Overview the study. Review the table of contents and read the study introduction. Try to see how each lesson relates to the overall study.

3. Use your Bible to read and consider prayerfully the Scripture passages for the lesson. (You'll see that each writer has chosen a favorite translation for the lessons in this issue. You're free to use the Bible translation you prefer and compare it with the translation chosen for that unit, of course.)

4. After reading all the Scripture passages in your Bible, then read the writer's comments. The comments are intended to be an aid to your study of the Bible.

5. Read the small articles—"sidebars"—in each lesson. They are intended to provide additional, enrichment information and inspiration and to encourage thought and application.

6. Try to answer for yourself the questions included in each lesson. They're intended to encourage further

thought and application, and they can also be used in the class session itself.

If you're the teacher—

Do all the things just mentioned, of course. As you begin the study with your class, be sure to find a way to help your class know the date on which each lesson will be studied. Here are some suggestions to guide your lesson preparation:

A. In the first session of the study, briefly overview the study by identifying for your class the date on which each lesson will be studied. Lead your class to write the date in the table of contents on pages 9–10 and on the first page of each lesson.

- Make and post a chart that indicates the date on which each lesson will be studied.
- If all your class has e-mail, send them an e-mail with the dates the lessons will be studied.
- Provide a bookmark with the lesson dates. You may want to include information about your church and then use the bookmark as an outreach tool, too. A model for a bookmark can be downloaded from www.baptistwaypress.org under the "Teacher Helps" menu.
- Develop a sticker with the lesson dates, and place it on the table of contents or on the back cover.

B. Get a copy of the *Teaching Guide*, a companion piece to this *Study Guide*. The *Teaching Guide* contains additional Bible comments plus two teaching plans. The teaching plans in the *Teaching Guide* are intended to provide practical, easy-to-use teaching suggestions that will work in your class.

C. After you've studied the Bible passage, the lesson comments, and other material, use the teaching suggestions in the *Teaching Guide* to help you develop your plan for leading your class in studying each lesson.

D. Teaching resource items for use as handouts are available free at www.baptistwaypress.org under the "Teacher Helps" tab.

E. Additional Bible study comments on the lessons are available online. Call 1–866–249–1799 or e-mail baptistway@texasbaptists.org to order the *Premium Commentary*. It is available only in electronic format (PDF) from our website, www.baptistwaypress.org. The price of these comments for the entire study is $5 per person. A church or class that participates in our advance order program for free shipping can receive the *Premium Commentary* free. Call 1–866–249–1799 or see www.baptistwaypress.org to purchase or for information on participating in our free shipping program for the next study.

F. Additional teaching plans are also available in electronic format (PDF) by calling 1–866–249–1799. The price of these additional teaching plans for the entire study is $5 per person. A church or class that participates in our advance order program for free shipping can receive the *Premium Teaching Plans* free. Call 1–866–249–1799 or see www.baptistwaypress.org for information on participating in our free shipping program for the next study.

G. Enjoy leading your class in discovering the meaning of the Scripture passages and in applying these passages to their lives.

Do you use a Kindle?

This Connect 360 *Bible Study Guide*, along with several other studies, is available in a Kindle edition. The easiest way to find these materials is to search for "BaptistWay" on your Kindle, or go to www.amazon.com/kindle and do a search for "BaptistWay." The Kindle edition can be studied not only on a Kindle but also on your smartphone or tablet using the Kindle app available free from amazon.com/kindle.

Writers for This *Study Guide*

Sharon Gritz wrote **lessons one through four.** A graduate of Southwestern Baptist Theological Seminary, she lives in Fort Worth, Texas, where she teaches Bible study at University Baptist Church and its mission, Luz del Mundo. She serves in the women's prayer ministry and a ready-for-school program for refugee children. Sharon's husband Paul is a retired professor of church history at Southwestern. Her daughter Lydia and son-in-law Taylor serve in an International Baptist Church in Germany.

Ed Jordan wrote **lessons five through seven.** Dr. Jordan is a graduate of Golden Gate Baptist Theological Seminary. He has written and edited a 52-lesson curriculum for new church plants and two hermeneutic books. He writes a weekly award-winning column for the Idaho State Journal, a quarterly column for the Danville Register & Bee's Southern Virginia Living Magazine, a weekly blog for the Baptist General Association of Virginia (BGAV.org), and a quarterly column for the BGAV Express. He and his wife live in Virginia where he serves as the pastor of Gwynn's Island Baptist Church.

Julie (Brown) Wood wrote **lessons eight through ten.** Julie is a graduate of Hardin-Simmons University and

Southwestern Baptist Theological Seminary. She loves ministering with her husband, Dr. Darin Wood, senior pastor of First Baptist Church in Midland, Texas; and being mother to their son, Joshua. A former children's minister and worship leader, she now serves in various volunteer capacities with her church and works as a free-lance writer and pianist.

Tom Howe wrote **lessons eleven through thirteen.** Tom recently became the Director of Urban Missions for Texas Baptists (BGCT). Prior to this new position he served as the senior pastor of Birdville Baptist Church, Haltom City, Texas. Dr. Howe is a graduate of East Texas Baptist University (B.S.), Beeson Divinity School at Samford University (M. Div.), and Southwestern Baptist Theological Seminary (D. Min.). He and his wife Amy have three children: Julia, Rhett and Grant.

Correction and Counsel
A Study of 1 & 2 Corinthians

1 CORINTHIANS
Questions, Problems, and Solutions

2 CORINTHIANS

Refute, Restore, and Raise Hope

Introducing

Correction and Counsel
A STUDY OF 1 & 2 CORINTHIANS

Teachers, coaches, employers, ministers, and parents often find themselves in the role of communicating correction and counsel to those for whom they are accountable. This is part of the responsibility of being a leader. The effectiveness of such instruction can often depend on the integrity of the leader and the condition of the relationship between the leader and those in need of the correction and counsel. As you may well know, sometimes these can be difficult conversations.

The Apostle Paul found himself in just such a situation with a church he had planted in Corinth during his second missionary journey. Corinth was a cosmopolitan city located on a major trade route, and happened to be one of the most wicked cities of the ancient world. It was famous for its pagan worship practices, especially the worship of the goddess Aphrodite. When it came to morality, Corinth was much like any large metropolitan city in the world today.

In the middle of this environment, these new church members (with many new converts from paganism), struggled with breaking the habits of their former lifestyles. Paul provide them with needed correction and counsel through the two letters we know as 1 and 2 Corinthians. He called them out for sinful practices, provided instruction regarding marriage, generosity, spiritual gifts, and church conflict, and wrote with eloquence regarding the true meaning of love. He also encouraged the Corinthians by reminding them they could live with resurrection hope and that God had promised his sufficient grace to meet their every need.

May we be encouraged as well to respond rightly to God's correction and counsel as revealed in the letters of 1 and 2 Corinthians. We can be confident that the words Jesus spoke to Paul are true for us as we seek to serve Christ in our world, "My grace is sufficient for you, for my power is made perfect in weakness" (2 Corinthians 12:9a, NIV).

Each fall our Connect 360 Bible Study series focuses on a New Testament offering. For a complete list our studies see www.baptistwaypress.org.

Background on 1 and 2 Corinthians[1]

From what we read in 1 and 2 Corinthians, the Christians at Corinth were a rowdy bunch. They had issues that divided them and that caused problems among themselves and in their witness to the world. They needed some strong guidance in getting back on the right track. Of course, that could never happen in your church today, could it?

A few years before the Corinthian letters were written, the missionary Paul had come to Corinth proclaiming the good news that people could rise above the despair and debauchery of their first-century world through the power of God. Unlike the gods whom the Corinthians had heard about before, this God had entered directly into human history. In fact, this God had come to live on earth for a brief time a few decades before in a man named Jesus.

This Jesus had taught the way of life and given himself sacrificially in death—the worst kind of death, crucifixion as a criminal. Moreover, somehow the meaning of Jesus' death extended to them, making them sense both the depth of their need and the greatness of God's grace. Jesus provided a way to live that meant joy and peace. He called them to follow him in witness and ministry. Even more, this Jesus had been resurrected from the dead! This unbelievable but true event assured them that God would raise those who followed Jesus to life after their death, too. The small group had been bonded together by the meaning and hope they had found in Jesus.

Then Paul had gone away. Uncertainty began to develop within the group, and people who had come into the group from various backgrounds began to try to answer the group's questions. Sometimes they tried to say what they thought Paul had really meant when he had said thus and so, and sometimes they tried to offer the religious and philosophical answers they had learned from the surrounding culture. Some of them were adamant in their statements of what they saw as the truth, even questioning, challenging, and rejecting Paul himself.

At the same time, some of the group evidently didn't get very far into the Christian faith. They began to return to the practices and patterns of life they had known in the past. They brought the kind of life they had known on the streets of Corinth into the life of the group. The consensus of at least some of the group was that living in such a manner was no problem now that they had become so spiritual.

Furthermore, bickering, disharmony, divisions, and quarreling began to characterize the group as people claimed to believe first this and then that. They formed cliques and parties based on what they thought they believed various human leaders—Paul, Apollos, Peter—had taught. Some even declared themselves to be above it all. They claimed that they simply followed Christ, looking down their first-century noses at the others.

Finally, someone suggested they should write Paul and ask him about the questions that were being raised. So they did, although the vote was far from unanimous. Perhaps the people who brought the letter to Paul—"Chloe's people"—also brought further news about what was really happening in the congregation (1 Corinthians 1:11).

So, Paul wrote the Corinthian Christians. In fact, he wrote several times. The church's problems were so great that one letter wouldn't do it. The letters that we have are our 1 and 2 Corinthians, and these letters are the basis for this study.

The Letters of 1 and 2 Corinthians in Our Day

The description of the challenges facing the church in Corinth sound as if they could be found in any number of churches today. Here are a few of the transferable principles:

1. **Divided Loyalties** . . . in the church often stem out of intellectual and spiritual pride, and can lead to disruption and division in the church.

2. **Immorality** . . . in the church must be addressed. To avoid doing so damages the church's witness and sends the wrong message to the world about following Christ. Church discipline must be applied as needed.

3. **Freedom** . . . must be exercised with responsibility. Just because something is permissible may not mean it is also beneficial. Christ-followers have a responsibility toward their brothers and sisters in Christ when it comes to matters of conscience.

4. **Worship** . . . must be conducted in an orderly manner, including the celebration of the Lord's Supper.

5. **Spiritual Gifts** . . . are all equally valuable, regardless of their characteristics, and are given to build up the church, the body of Christ.

6. **Resurrection Hope** . . . Paul proclaimed the reality of this event and the hope that believers can live with based on the certainty of Christ's resurrection.

7. **Trials** . . . Christ's grace is sufficient to meet our every need as we suffer trials.

8. **Generosity** . . . We have been blessed to be a blessing to others. Our generosity proves we view ourselves as stewards of God's blessings rather than "owners."[2]

The letters of 1 and 2 Corinthians provide many points of application for our personal lives as well as for the lives and ministries of our churches. Our prayer is that this study will challenge and encourage you through the loving correction and counsel of God's word.

1 CORINTHIANS: QUESTIONS, PROBLEMS, AND SOLUTIONS

Additional Resources for Studying *Correction and Counsel*[3]

Kenneth L. Barker and John R. Kohlenberger III. *The Expositor's Bible Commentary—Abridged Edition: New Testament*. Grand Rapids, Michigan: Zondervan, 1994.

Paul Barnett. *The Second Epistle to the Corinthians*. The New International Commentary on the New Testament. Grand Rapids, Michigan: William B. Eerdmans Publishing Company, 1997.

Bruce Barton, Philip Comfort, Grant Osborne, Linda K. Taylor, and Dave Veerman. *Life Application New Testament Commentary*. Carol Stream, Illinois: Tyndale House Publishers, Inc., 2001.

G.R. Beasley-Murray. "2 Corinthians." *The Broadman Bible Commentary*. Volume 11. Nashville, Tennessee: Broadman Press, 1971.

Ernest Best. *Second Corinthians*. Interpretation: A Bible Commentary for Teaching and Preaching. Louisville: John Knox Press, 1987.

Raymond Bryan Brown. "1 Corinthians." *Broadman Bible Commentary*. Volume 10. Nashville, Tennessee: Broadman Press, 1970.

F.F. Bruce. *1 and 2 Corinthians*. New Century Bible. London: Oliphants, 1971.

Kenneth L. Chafin. *1, 2 Corinthians*. The Communicator's Commentary. Waco, Texas: Word Books, Publisher, 1985.

David Garland. *2 Corinthians*. The New American Commentary. Nashville, Tennessee: Broadman and Holman, 1999.

_____. *1 Corinthians*. Baker Exegetical Commentary on the New Testament. Grand Rapids, Michigan: Baker Academic, 2003.

Brian Harbour. *2 Corinthians: Commissioned to Serve*. Nashville, Tennessee: Convention Press, 1989.

Fred D. Howard. *1 Corinthians: Guidelines for God's People*. Nashville, Tennessee: Convention Press, 1983.

Craig S. Keener. *1 and 2 Corinthians*. New Cambridge Bible Commentary. New York: Cambridge University Press, 2005.

J.W. MacGorman. *Romans, 1 Corinthians*. The Layman's Bible Book Commentary. Volume 20. Nashville: Broadman Press, 1980.

John B. Polhill. *Paul and His Letters*. Nashville, Tennessee: Broadman and Holman Publishers, 1999.

A.T. Robertson. *Word Pictures in the New Testament*. Volume IV. Nashville, Tennessee: Broadman Press, 1931.

J. Paul Sampley. "The Second Letter to the Corinthians." *The New Interpreter's Bible*. Volume XI. Nashville: Abingdon Press, 2000.

NOTES

1. This background information first appeared in the introductory material of *Letters to the Corinthian Church: Imperatives for an Imperfect Church*, 2011, BaptistWay Press.

2. Barton, Comfort, Osborne, Taylor, and Veerman, 646–49, 709–10.

3. Listing a book does not imply full agreement by the writers or BAPTISTWAY PRESS® with all of its comments.

Introducing 1 Corinthians

Questions, Problems, and Solutions

"Questions, Problems, and Solutions" serves as an outline to describe the Book of 1 Corinthians. In this letter to the church he planted in Corinth, Paul addressed several issues. Lesson one explores how the gospel confounds human wisdom, and lesson two shows how spiritual immaturity can lead to factions in the church. Lesson three reveals why the church must confront cultural compromise among her members, and lesson four advises Christians to seek the good of others as they exercise their freedom in Christ. Lesson five explains the nature and purpose of spiritual gifts, while lesson six describes true, biblical love. Lesson seven provides a word of encouragement for living in confident hope because of Jesus' resurrection.

1 CORINTHIANS: QUESTIONS, PROBLEMS, AND SOLUTIONS

lesson  1

The Cross: Wisdom or Foolishness?

MAIN IDEA

The gospel confounds human wisdom.

QUESTION TO EXPLORE

Why does the gospel seem like foolishness to some people?

STUDY AIM

To place my trust in God's wisdom and the provision of the cross

QUICK READ

Paul explained how the gospel message seems foolish to most people and how those who respond to its call look foolish to the world. The gospel confounds human wisdom.

Introduction

I've seen multiple television shows that present smart people—geniuses—as miracle-working problem-solvers. The brainy person saves the day by preventing a catastrophe or rescuing lives in an impossible situation. Also, numerous movies depict superheroes who rescue people and the world from disaster. These media declare that human effort—brain power or special abilities—can overcome any difficulty and save us. They display the world's wisdom and its idea of a savior.

The gospel offers a wholly different image of a Savior: a crucified Messiah despised and rejected by others, whose life portrayed sorrow and terrible suffering. Most of Jesus' contemporaries thought of him as a "nobody" and viewed his actions as impudent and foolish. Today, many continue to label the gospel as foolishness. Why? The gospel confounds human wisdom. It does not appear to make sense. However, the Servant who suffered on the cross became the resurrected, living, exalted Lord. Only he can actually rescue people and save the world from disaster. Placing our trust in God's wisdom and the provision of the cross is the best—and wisest—action we can take. The Apostle Paul helps us to understand this truth.

Understanding the Context of 1 Corinthians

Occasionally, I hear Christians say, "We need to be a New Testament church." However, I have never heard someone say, "We need to be like the church at Corinth." The Corinthian church had heaps of problems. Paul's letters to that immature congregation, however, help us learn how to be the Lord's people in today's world.

Paul arrived at Corinth in the early A.D. 50s on his second missionary journey (Acts 18:1–18). [See sidebar: "A Picture of Corinth."] As was his custom, the apostle first preached in the synagogue. The synagogue ruler, Crispus, and his household believed the gospel. Jewish opposition, however, led Paul to focus his ministry on the Gentiles. Those converts to the Christian faith brought into the church their Greek-Roman worldview and attitude toward moral behavior. Both slaves and freedmen joined the new group of believers, yet the congregation also included the wealthy, such as Erastus, Corinth's city treasurer (Romans 16:23). Paul spent eighteen months in Corinth until Jewish persecution forced him to leave.

Before writing 1 Corinthians, Paul had already written a letter to the church at Corinth (see 1 Cor. 5:9–11). That first letter encouraged the believers not to associate with those who claimed to be believers yet indulged in sin. The apostle was in Ephesus on his third missionary journey. Some members of the Corinthian congregation from Chloe's household had come to Paul with a report, informing him of problems among the Corinthian believers (1:11; 5:1; 11:18). The apostle also received a letter from the church that asked specific questions (7:1).

In response to the oral reports and the letter from Corinth, Paul wrote 1 Corinthians from Ephesus in the spring of A.D. 54 or 55 to help the believers at Corinth know how to live for Christ in a pagan, corrupt society. The apostle wrote to correct their wrong practices, answer their questions, and offer correct teachings about the resurrection.

After his usual greetings and thanksgiving for the Corinthians, Paul addressed the factions in the church. From 1:18 to 4:21, the apostle tackled the causes of the divisions. He contended the schisms were birthed from an over-estimation of human wisdom and unfounded pride about the makeup of the Corinthian Christian community.

1 Corinthians 1:18–31

18 For the word of the cross is foolishness to those who are perishing, but to us who are being saved it is the power of God. **19** For it is written,

"I WILL DESTROY THE WISDOM OF THE WISE,

AND THE CLEVERNESS OF THE CLEVER I WILL SET ASIDE."

20 Where is the wise man? Where is the scribe? Where is the debater of this age? Has not God made foolish the wisdom of the world? **21** For since in the wisdom of God the world through its wisdom did not *come to* know God, God was well-pleased through the foolishness of the message preached to save those who believe. **22** For indeed Jews ask for signs and Greeks search for wisdom; **23** but we preach Christ crucified, to Jews a stumbling block and to Gentiles foolishness, **24** but to those who are the called, both Jews and Greeks, Christ the power of God and the wisdom of God. **25** Because the foolishness of God is wiser than men, and the weakness of God is stronger than men.

26 For consider your calling, brethren, that there were not many wise according to the flesh, not many mighty, not many noble; **27** but God has chosen the foolish things of the world to shame the wise, and God has chosen the weak things of the world to shame the things which are strong, **28** and the base things of the world and the despised God has chosen, the things that are not, so that He may nullify the things that are, **29** so that no man may boast before God. **30** But by His doing you are in Christ Jesus, who became to us wisdom from God, and righteousness and sanctification, and redemption, **31** so that, just as it is written, "LET HIM WHO BOASTS, BOAST IN THE LORD."

Understanding the Foolishness of the Gospel's Message (1:18–25)

The dictionary defines "foolishness" as *silliness, stupidity, absurdity, or ridiculousness*. Paul used a form of this word five times in eight verses. In the first century, many viewed the word of the cross, that is, the gospel message, as foolishness. The cross had a negative meaning in that era. It referred to a despised and cruel manner of death, a punishment for criminals and rebels. Why would anyone want to embrace a Savior who had endured such a shameful death? Still, God chose the cross as the means of salvation for sinful humanity. He transformed a symbol of terror and humiliation into one of love and power.

The Apostle Paul affirmed that the cross divides humanity into two groups: the perishing and the saved. Those who view the cross as nonsense are on the path of ultimate disaster. For believers, however, the cross is the power of God. Through the cross, God defeated evil, made his love known, and redeemed sinners. Rather than brash foolishness, the cross represents absolute power.

To support his argument, Paul quoted Isaiah 29:14 to show that God destroys and sets aside human wisdom as a means of salvation. He does not need human help to accomplish his plan of salvation. In Isaiah's day, the political cleverness of Jerusalem's leaders failed. Their human wisdom ("Ask Egypt for help.") prompted the exact thing they wanted to prevent—Assyrian invasion (2 Kings 18:13–25).

Paul used a series of rhetorical questions to emphasize his point (v. 20). He was saying, "Where are all the experts—the wise man, scribe, and debater of this age? Can these professionals do what the cross has done?" God makes those who think they have all the answers look foolish. The phrase "of this age" extends to the experts of the present age whom God has judged; their watery wisdom is also passing away. The humble and self-sacrificing wisdom of the cross also dominates that of experts in generations to come. Paul was not rejecting the use of intellect, but he warned of a prideful and self-serving mindset.

God saves those who believe. In his wisdom, God planned for people to come to him through faith. Human reasoning or effort cannot bring individuals into a relationship with God. The wording "well-pleased" refers to God's free and sovereign choice in salvation. God chooses to use "the foolishness of the message preached"—a crucified Savior. Salvation does not come through human wisdom but from Jesus Christ's "foolish" (in the world's opinion) death on a cross. God's wisdom makes salvation available to all people.

The Jews knew God's past mighty acts on their behalf. They expected a political Messiah who would perform those "signs." They wanted visual proof, refusing to trust. Instead, Jesus gave them the sign of Jonah (Matthew 12:39–40) as a testament to his death and resurrection. The Greeks rejected that and chose instead to search for wisdom, wanting to find God through the power of human reasoning.

In contrast, Paul preached "Christ crucified." A crucified Messiah was a "stumbling block," a scandal to the Jews because anyone who hung on a tree was cursed (Galatians 3:13). The crucified Christ did not fit their model of an exalted, victorious king. To the Gentiles, the idea of anyone who died a criminal's death on the cross being a Savior was "foolish." Only those whom God calls, both Jews and Greeks, understand the true meaning of Christ crucified as "the power of God and the wisdom of God." God's power and wisdom save.

This "foolishness of God"—saving humanity through the death of his Son on the cross—is wiser than any human wisdom. This "weakness of God"—allowing Jesus to die, taking the penalty of sin for undeserving sinners—is stronger than any human strength. Human wisdom and power fail to rescue people from sin and its punishment. God's supposed foolishness and weakness are the only way to salvation.

Why does the gospel appear as foolishness to many today? It is not the way humans would have done it! Don't we prefer to do things our way, without any help? People still respond to the gospel either by stumbling, laughing, or believing. God calls us to trust in his wisdom—even if it contradicts the wisdom of the world and even if we don't understand it.

Understanding the Foolishness of the Gospel's Recipients (1:26–31)

Churches sometimes develop a character or reputation based on the composition of their membership, such as the professionals' church, cowboy church, multi-ethnic church, mega-church, and millennials' church. Paul turned his attention to the makeup of the church at Corinth. Pagan outsiders would have viewed the unimportance of the Corinthian believers as another example of the gospel's foolishness.

The apostle encouraged the Corinthians to consider what they were when God called them to salvation—and still were. Most of them had no significant standing in society.

Not many of them were considered "wise"—educated and clever. Not many were "mighty," holding positions of power and influence. Not many were "noble," born into the elite families of the wealthy, ruling class. By human standards, the Corinthians were unintelligent, weak, and unimportant. Salvation is not, however, based on human criteria. God's call is grace-based.

By repeating the words "God has chosen" three times (vv. 27–28), Paul emphasized God's sovereignty in salvation. God chooses "the foolish things, the weak things, the base and despised, and the things that are not." From the world's viewpoint, these are the "nobodies" of society. God's choice "shamed" the "wise," the "strong," and the "somebodies" of the world. The wise think the cross is a ridiculous way to save the world. The strong believe they are self-sustaining and have no need for God to rescue them. The noble will not lower themselves to follow a crucified Savior. The word *shamed* in this context refers to coming under God's judgment. God reverses the values of the world. He uses what the world classifies as worthless, useless, and zilch to nullify (destroy) what the world values. The self-proclaimed elite can do nothing to save themselves regardless of their wisdom, power, and influence.

Paul explained the purpose of God's plan in choosing the foolish, weak, and despised: so that no person "may boast before God." We cannot brag that our efforts merit a right relationship with God. Our salvation depends on God's call, his choosing—his grace. God chooses those who have nothing to brag about—humble seekers. And he receives all the glory.

God's work alone gives believers new life, uniting them with Christ Jesus, who became to us wisdom from God. The Apostle Paul explained the fruits of this wisdom or salvation. The word *righteousness* means Christ's work on the cross enables us to have a right relationship with God, ourselves, and others. Jesus shares with us his righteous character. *Sanctification* means that through Christ, God sets us apart, makes us holy, and allows us into his holy presence. The character of Christ is being formed in us. *Redemption* means Christ's death on the cross purchased our freedom from slavery to sin, as well as its power and penalty. Paul quoted from Jeremiah 9:23–24. If we want to boast, we should boast only in the Lord and his redemptive work on our behalf.

Are you boasting in what the Lord has done for you?

Implications and Actions

Two hymns came to my mind as I studied 1 Corinthians 1: "When I Survey the Wondrous Cross" by Isaac Watts and "The Old Rugged Cross" by George Bennard. These two hymns reflect an understanding of verses 18–31. The cross is not foolishness. It is the center of the gospel message, representing the supreme event of human history. The cross makes God's gift of salvation unique and powerful. It gives us hope and confidence. Though the world views it as the emblem of suffering and shame, we should love and cherish the cross and proclaim its message to all those who are perishing.

The power of the cross transforms broken lives. It gives fresh life and a new direction. It provides a valid reason for boasting. The cross signifies how God's grace offers salvation freely. Every person comes to God through faith in the crucified—yet risen—Christ.

The cross indeed confounds human wisdom. Will you place your trust in God's wisdom and his provision of the cross? Will you boast only in the death of Christ our Lord and pour contempt on all your pride? Let's cling to that old rugged cross.

A Picture of Corinth

Corinth flourished as a Greek city for centuries until the Roman Lucius Mummius destroyed it in 146 B.C. After remaining ruined and mostly uninhabited, Julius Caesar rebuilt Corinth as a Roman colony in 44 B.C. and colonized the city with freed slaves, soldiers, and urban laborers. The rebuilt Corinth soon regained the importance it had once possessed as a Greek city and served as the capital of the Roman province of Achaia. With two harbors, its strategic location on the Isthmus of Greece made it a major, wealthy trade center.

Corinth's population was diverse and transient with many cultures and religions. The city became a center of art, philosophy, and religion. Corinth had many pagan temples, including those of Apollo, the Greek god of music, truth, and prophecy, as well as Aphrodite, the goddess of love. In the first century A.D., Corinth was an active, proud, and intellectual city with immigrants from far and wide. Also, as with many seaports and commercial cities of its time, immorality flourished.

Case Study

Mike is a brilliant businessman, inventor, investor, and philanthropist. His intellect has led to a net worth in the billions. Mike does whatever he wants to do. He enjoys life and lives it to the fullest with enthusiasm. Mike does not practice or embrace any religious beliefs. Why would the gospel seem like foolishness to Mike? Why would the cross offend his pride? How would you communicate the gospel to Mike?

Questions

1. Our culture worships power, influence, popularity, wealth, brains, and beauty. How can these idols become a barrier to placing trust in Jesus as Savior and Lord?

2. Why does the cross of Christ offend our pride? How does the message of Christ crucified prevent us from boasting of personal triumphs in the presence of God?

3. Why is the message of the cross foolishness to those who are perishing? How should this guide our evangelism efforts?

4. How does the cross make salvation available to all people, leveling the playing field?

5. Why does God choose those who have nothing to brag about but him? What does this say about God's character?

NOTES

1. Unless otherwise indicated, all Scripture quotations in lessons 1–10 are from the New American Standard Bible (1995 edition).

lesson 2

Spiritual Maturity: The Cure for Church Conflict

MAIN IDEA

A lack of spiritual maturity can lead to factions in the church.

QUESTION TO EXPLORE

What is the cure for church conflict?

STUDY AIM

To evaluate my level of spiritual maturity and its impact on my church

QUICK READ

Paul confronted the Corinthians about their spiritual immaturity which had fostered factions in the church, corrected their misunderstanding regarding church leaders, and warned of the danger of destroying the church.

Introduction

Kay told me why she left her former church family. The church planned to relocate and construct a new facility. Some church members favored having all the funds in the bank before the building project began to avoid debt. Others wanted to take advantage of low-interest rates and borrow the money. Business meetings became angry arguments between the two sides. The critical moment for Kay came when it was time to vote by ballot on what action to take. When the moderator appointed a deacon to help count the votes, another member shouted, "I don't trust him to count the votes. He's on the other side."

Like Kay, I have witnessed painful conflicts in church families. How we must grieve God. Jesus prayed for the unity of believers, including us—his future disciples (John 17:20–21). He understands our nature. Spiritual immaturity can lead to factions in the church. What is the cure for such church conflict? Spiritual maturity. Paul confronted the Corinthians with their immaturity and warned them of the danger of destroying the church.

1 Corinthians 3:1–17

1 And I, brethren, could not speak to you as to spiritual men, but as to men of flesh, as to infants in Christ. **2** I gave you milk to drink, not solid food; for you were not yet able *to receive* *it.* Indeed, even now you are not yet able, **3** for you are still fleshly. For since there is jealousy and strife among you, are you not fleshly, and are you not walking like mere men? **4** For when one says, "I am of Paul," and another, "I am of Apollos," are you not *mere* men?

5 What then is Apollos? And what is Paul? Servants through whom you believed, even as the Lord gave *opportunity* to each one. **6** I planted, Apollos watered, but God was causing the growth. **7** So then neither the one who plants nor the one who waters is anything, but God who causes the growth. **8** Now he who plants and he who waters are one; but each will receive his own reward according to his own labor. **9** For we are God's fellow workers; you are God's field, God's building.

10 According to the grace of God which was given to me, like a wise master builder I laid a foundation, and another is building on it. But each man must be careful how he builds on it. **11** For no man can lay a foundation other than the one which is laid, which is Jesus Christ. **12** Now if any man builds on the foundation with gold, silver, precious stones, wood, hay, straw, **13** each man's work will become evident; for the day will show it because it is *to be* revealed with fire, and the fire itself will test the quality of each man's work. **14** If any man's work which he has built on it remains, he will receive a reward. **15** If any man's work is burned up, he will suffer loss; but he himself will be saved, yet so as through fire.

16 Do you not know that you are a temple of God and *that* the Spirit of God dwells in you? **17** If any man destroys the temple of God, God will destroy him, for the temple of God is holy, and that is what you are.

Mature Believers Don't Act Like the World (3:1–4)

Babies often bring a smile to our faces. We delight in their sweet innocence. Most parents enjoy those baby years, and some are sad when they end. No one, however, wants these little persons to remain babies! We are supposed to grow and mature—physically and spiritually.

Paul confronted the Corinthians about their spiritual immaturity as revealed in the divisions among them (1 Cor. 1:10–13). The apostle had indirectly addressed this problem by correcting their view of the gospel of Christ crucified (1:18–31—2:1–5) and explaining how the Spirit reveals God's wisdom (2:6–16). Paul wanted to correct their misunderstanding of church leaders and the church.

During the apostle's initial visit to Corinth, the new converts were "infants in Christ." The Holy Spirit dwelled in them, but they were not spiritually mature. Instead, they were persons of flesh or "fleshly," controlled by their human desires rather than the Spirit. They were living and thinking like people who did not have the Spirit.

As young, immature believers, Paul gave them "milk to drink, not solid food." The apostle used the Corinthians' own words. They had accused Paul of preaching only milk and not the solid food of the worldly substitutes (human wisdom) they preferred. However, the apostle had preached the gospel—which was both milk and solid food. The church at Corinth did not need a different diet. They needed a different attitude about the gospel of the crucified Christ instead of dismissing God's wisdom as foolishness.

Ironically, the Corinthian believers boasted of their spiritual giftedness, but their behavior reflected immaturity and worldliness: "jealousy and strife." Jealousy and strife (or rivalry) are works of the flesh (Galatians 5:20). They spring from self-centeredness and pride. The Corinthians were worldly, walking like unspiritual people (the natural person Paul described in 1 Cor. 2:14). They did not show life in the Spirit.

The Corinthians had divided into factions over several teachers, including Paul and Apollos. [See sidebar "The Bio of Apollos."] Paul quoted some of their party slogans, "I am of Paul" and "I am of Apollos," to emphasize their spiritual immaturity. By taking sides, they were acting like people who belonged to the world, not to Christ.

Do you quarrel like children and take sides in your church family? Immature believers allow their desires to control them. Don't stunt your spiritual growth. Let the Holy Spirit direct your life.

Mature Believers Recognize God's Ownership (3:5–9)

"The Texas Rangers will beat the Houston Astros!" If you live in Texas, you might hear such a statement—or its opposite. It's fine to compare sports teams. Believers, however, should not compare pastors or follow these leaders instead of following Jesus Christ. Mature believers recognize that all church leaders, as well as all believers, belong to God as his servants.

The apostle identified himself and Apollos as "servants" who belonged to God, their Master. Each did the task assigned to him by God. The word *servant* denotes one who does the lowliest task. The status-seeking Corinthians would have viewed this idea as disgusting. Paul's words "through whom" indicate these leaders served as God's instruments to guide the Corinthians to mature faith.

Paul used a farming metaphor, depicting himself and Apollos as field hands, laborers in the field. He "planted," meaning he introduced the Corinthians to the gospel message. "Apollos watered," meaning he continued instructing them in the truths of the faith. Both jobs were important and necessary for the growth of the church. The active phrase is "but God was causing the growth."

The Lord gets the credit. Without him, no growth would take place, despite the planting and watering of the servants. Paul was instructing the Corinthians to stop over-emphasizing the efforts of humans in the ministry of the gospel. Those who plant and those who water point others to Christ, not to themselves. God causes the growth. Why were the Corinthians quarreling over servants whose work is nothing compared to God, who alone can save? God is everything.

Paul stressed the unity of God's workers—they "are one." Though united in purpose, God considers them accountable as individuals. God will reward each worker "according to his own labor." The apostle did not identify the nature of the reward. God rewards the quality of one's labor—not the success of the assigned task (as humans tend to judge).

Paul emphasized God's ownership by repeating the possessive word "God's" three times (v. 9). All belong to God: Paul, Apollos, and the church ("field, building"). The expression "fellow workers" means that Paul and Apollos worked together under God's leadership. The apostle used two images for the church. "Field" continued his agricultural metaphor. "Building" introduced an architectural metaphor.

As believers, we belong to God. We are his servants. We all have different jobs in God's field. We need each other to fulfill the Lord's work. Immature believers focus more on human leaders and themselves than on God. Mature believers recognize God's ownership and surrender to his will for their lives.

Are you immature or mature?

Mature Believers Expect God's Testing (3:10–15)

We encounter testing throughout our lives: school assessments, medical examinations, employee evaluations. Paul told the Corinthians—and all believers—that God will test their service for him. We are accountable to God.

Paul developed the building metaphor of the church. God appointed him a "wise master builder." The word *wise* (Greek, *sophos*) means "skilled," or "expert," but the apostle chose this term to rebuke the Corinthians' obsession with human wisdom (Greek, *sophia*). Paul could not take any credit for who he was or what he had accomplished. God's "grace" had enabled all of it.

As the building contractor, the Apostle Paul knew the only "foundation" possible was "Jesus Christ." Paul preached and taught the gospel of the cross and its crucified Messiah. Others, such as Apollos, built on that foundation with teachings related to the same gospel. The general words such as "another, each man," and "no man" enable Paul's words to apply not only to teachers, but to every believer who serves the Lord. All of us "must be careful" how we build on this foundation, emphasizing the quality of our service, not quantity. We should find our area of service and do it well.

Paul noted two types of building materials used for the structure placed on the foundation: the valuable and imperishable (lasting), as opposed to the worthless and perishable. When Christ returns on "the day," each person's "work will become evident." "The day" refers to the end-time judgment. The "fire" of God's judgment will reveal and "test the quality" of each person's work. Only durable materials will survive this testing. Those who have built well, whose work "remains," will "receive a reward," the wage earned for quality work. Those who have built with useless materials will "suffer loss" of pay just like those who must pay fines for inferior work. The result of this judgment is a loss of reward, not a loss of salvation. Such individuals "will be saved," but like someone barely escaping through a wall of flames. Their work, however, will not survive. Although Paul did not define the nature of this reward, he affirmed its certainty.

Are you expecting God's testing of your service for him? Quality materials include a servant heart, making disciples, and loving others as you love yourself. Inferior materials include self-centeredness, stinginess, and serving the Lord in your own strength. What materials are you using? Will they survive God's judgment?

Mature Believers Build Up the Church (3:16–17)

Most mornings I walk through my neighborhood. It impresses me how many workers it takes to remodel an old house or build a new home. Spiritually, it requires a group of believers to build up the church. All of us have a God-given role in the construction process.

The Apostle Paul reminded the Corinthians they were God's "temple." The usage of the pronoun *you* in this passage is plural—the Corinthians together were God's temple. Paul used the Greek word for *temple,* referring to the shrine or sanctuary where the deity dwells. The church at Corinth was a dwelling for God because the "Spirit of God dwells in you." The Spirit's presence in their midst marked them as God's temple and served as the source of their unity. The Lord God did not need a physical temple in Corinth; the gathered believers formed his dwelling place.

Paul gave a severe warning: "If any person destroys the temple of God, God will destroy him." The Corinthians were in danger of destroying God's temple from within with their pride, interest in worldly wisdom, and factions. Anyone guilty of such an action would merit a punishment fit for the crime. Paul did not explain the meaning of "God will destroy him." Perhaps the apostle left this vague to strengthen his warning. Punishment was necessary because God's temple is holy, set apart. His people should also be holy since they belong to him.

When we gather together as the church, we are God's holy of holies, his dwelling place. God values the local church. We are not to mess with it. Mature believers support, strengthen, and build up the church. Do your actions show you value the church?

Implications and Actions

Paul's message to the first-century church at Corinth is relevant for us today. Sadly, most of us know about churches in conflict. The apostle would tell us what he told the Corinthians, "You are acting like babies! Grow up!" Yes, my side/your-side mentality reveals our spiritual immaturity. Spiritual maturity cures church divisions.

Mature believers don't act like the world—like those who do not know Christ. We allow the Holy Spirit to direct our thoughts, words, and actions—not our sinful natures. Mature believers recognize God's ownership of ourselves and our fellow Christians. We are all his servants—including all ministers and lay leaders. All glory should go to the one Master whom we serve.

Mature believers should expect God's testing of our service for him. We are accountable to God. We should build his church with quality materials and quality work, giving our best efforts. Finally, mature believers build up the church. We do not tear it down with gossip, criticism, bitterness, and anger. We work together with fellow church members to cultivate God's field and build God's building.

What is your level of spiritual maturity, and how is it impacting your church?

The Bio of Apollos

Apollos was a Jew, a native of Alexandria, Egypt—the city of learning in the Greco-Roman world—and a gifted speaker (Acts 18:24–28). He knew the Old Testament Scriptures thoroughly. Although Apollos had been instructed in the way of the Lord and taught others the facts about Jesus, he only knew the baptism of John. Bible scholars debate what that means. When Apollos spoke boldly in the synagogue in Ephesus, Priscilla and Aquila recognized he needed further instruction. They took him aside and explained the way of God to him more accurately.

When Apollos decided to go to Achaia, the Ephesian church provided a letter of introduction. In Corinth, Apollos strengthened the believers by his skillful preaching. His Scripture knowledge enabled him to present compelling arguments proving Jesus was the Messiah and equipped him to publicly refute the Jews. His expert public speaking and education impressed many of the Corinthians, causing some to say, "I follow Apollos." Apollos returned to Ephesus and was with Paul when he wrote 1 Corinthians (see 16:12).

Are You Mature or Immature?

What most characterizes you: your sinful nature's desires or the Spirit's fruit? Study the lists below.

Signs of immaturity: sexual immorality, impurity, lustful pleasures, idolatry, sorcery, hostility, quarreling, jealousy, outbursts of anger, selfish ambition, dissension, division, envy, drunkenness, wild parties (Galatians 5:18–21).

Signs of maturity: love, joy, peace, patience, kindness, goodness, faithfulness, gentleness, self-control, mercy, forgiveness (Gal. 5:22–23; Ephesians 4:32).

Immature believers ignore sins or refuse to deal with them. Mature believers daily commit their sinful tendencies to God's control and seek the Holy Spirit's power to overcome them.

What are you doing?

Questions

1. Are you a spiritual infant, child, teenager, or adult? How can you begin to change your attitudes and actions so that you can grow in your maturity?

2. What are some evidences of spiritual immaturity in your life? In your church?

3. Why do factions develop in some churches? What is the cure for such factions?

4. In what ways are you contributing to the spiritual health and maturity of your church?

5. Do you see yourself as God's servant, called to make disciples and partner with fellow believers to accomplish God's work? Why or why not?

6. Which of your works for the Lord will burn to a crisp in eternity? Which works will stand the test of time? How can you ensure more of your works will pass through the fire?

lesson  3

Confronting Cultural Compromise

MAIN IDEA

The church must confront, and not condone, cultural compromise among its members.

QUESTION TO EXPLORE

How should the church confront cultural compromise among its members?

STUDY AIM

To identify how I can confront cultural compromise in my church

QUICK READ

Paul rebuked the Corinthians for boasting about an incestuous man in the church instead of expelling him. The church must confront, not condone, cultural compromise among its members.

Introduction

Jim and Tammy Faye Bakker illustrate the dangers of compromising with our culture. In the 1970s and 1980s, these televangelists built a Christian entertainment empire. The couple launched a satellite network a year before ESPN began broadcasting. They hosted a popular, televised Christian talk show, the PTL (Praise the Lord) Club. They built a Christian theme park, Heritage USA. The Bakkers embraced the prosperity gospel and encouraged their followers to believe that God wanted them to be happy and prosperous.

As leaders of their Heritage Village Church, the Bakkers appeared to have no accountability. Their private sins, however, became public and brought their downfall. Their offenses included sexual misconduct, greed, fraud, self-indulgence (lavish lifestyle), and deceit. This ministry team conformed to our culture's materialistic, self-serving values. In 1987, the Assemblies of God dismissed Jim Bakker for conduct unbecoming of a minister.

We know the Bakkers are not alone in compromising with our society. Christians—both ministers and laypeople—continue to yield to the temptations surrounding us. Paul's letter to the church at Corinth gives us a timely reminder: The church must confront, and not condone, cultural compromise among its members.

1 Corinthians 5

1 It is actually reported that there is immorality among you, and immorality of such a kind as does not exist even among the Gentiles, that someone has his father's wife. **2** You have become arrogant and have not mourned instead, so that the one who had done this deed would be removed from your midst.

3 For I, on my part, though absent in body but present in spirit, have already judged him who has so committed this, as though I were present. **4** In the name of our Lord Jesus, when you are assembled, and I with you in spirit, with the power of our Lord Jesus, **5** *I have decided* to deliver such a one to Satan for the destruction of his flesh, so that his spirit may be saved in the day of the Lord Jesus.

6 Your boasting is not good. Do you not know that a little leaven leavens the whole lump *of dough*? **7** Clean out the old leaven so that you may be a new lump, just as you are *in fact* unleavened. For Christ our Passover also has been sacrificed. **8** Therefore let us celebrate the feast, not with old leaven, nor with the leaven of malice and wickedness, but with the unleavened bread of sincerity and truth.

9 I wrote you in my letter not to associate with immoral people; **10** I *did* not at all *mean* with the immoral people of this world, or with the covetous and swindlers, or with idolaters, for then you would have to go out of the world. **11** But actually, I wrote to you not to associate with any so-called brother if he is an immoral person, or covetous, or an idolater, or a reviler, or a drunkard, or a swindler—not even to eat with such a one. **12** For what have I to do with judging outsiders? Do you not judge those who are within *the church*? **13** But those who are outside, God judges. REMOVE THE WICKED MAN FROM AMONG YOURSELVES.

Identify Cultural Compromise (5:1–2)

A medical doctor must analyze symptoms to identify a health problem. In the same manner, a church cannot confront cultural compromise among its members until it recognizes the compromising sin. Paul identified two evils among the Corinthian believers: incest and pride.

The apostle heard a report of sexual immorality in the church at Corinth that shocked and horrified him. Although the Greek word *porneia* refers to sexual wrongdoing of any kind, the context indicates that Paul referred to incest. A church member was sleeping with his stepmother. Sexual immorality of all types characterized the Greco-Roman world, but even pagans prohibited incest. This man engaged in behavior appalling to unbelievers who did not have high sexual standards. This scandal harmed the Christian witness to the pagan world. Since Paul did not rebuke the woman, she probably was not a believer.

Paul then focused on the second sin. The Corinthians had become arrogant and proud of themselves, literally "puffed up." The apostle had previously accused them of their spiritual pride (1 Cor. 4:6, 18–19). In verse six, Paul used the related word "boasting," recalling previous uses of self-aggrandizement (1:29, 31; 3:21; 4:7). He continued with condemnation of a specific instance of pride. Instead of arrogance, the Corinthians should have "mourned" in sorrow and shame. Tolerating this sin among them implicated the whole Christian community. They had allowed God's holy temple—the church—to be polluted. They should have removed this man from their fellowship.

Why were these believers proud of an incestuous relationship by one of their church members? Perhaps they viewed the guilty man as flaunting his freedom in Christ—freedom from Jewish and Gentile laws. Some heretical teachings in the early church believed Christians were spiritual persons so they could do whatever they wanted with their bodies. Or, perhaps this immoral man had a prominent place in the church as a leader or financial patron. The church did not want to offend him. So, they ignored the sin. At any rate, the Corinthians themselves were sinning in their attitude toward the situation and their failure to take corporate action. Paul wanted to deflate their excessive pride.

Have you identified cultural compromise in your church family? Are these unplanned errors or brazen sins? Do you think your church ignores these sins? Why or why not?

Take Action Against Cultural Compromise (5:3–5)

After a medical doctor has diagnosed a condition and prescribed treatment, one must take action to follow that plan. Paul took action against the sinner in the Corinthian congregation.

In contrast to the church at Corinth, which had done nothing, Paul passed judgment on the offender. Although the apostle was not with the Corinthians physically, he was present with them in spirit. The presence of the Holy Spirit in both Paul and the believers at Corinth united them. When the church assembled, Paul was present because of this unity. The verb form of *already judged* stresses the finality of the apostle's sentence—the guilty man still stood judged as the Corinthians read the apostle's letter. Paul, along with the gathered church, could carry out such judgment with the full authority of Jesus as indicated by the phrases "in the name of our Lord Jesus" and "with the power of our Lord Jesus."

The action Paul took revealed the seriousness of the sin: He delivered the man to Satan for the destruction of his flesh. By throwing this member out of the church fellowship, he was turned back into Satan's realm and excluded from the believing community with its life in the Spirit. Some interpreters view the destruction of his flesh as referring to the man's physical body. He might experience severe illness or death. Job suffered physically at Satan's hand (Job 2). Ananias and Sapphira died because they lied to the Holy Spirit (Acts 5:1–11).

Other interpreters view the word *flesh* as *sinful nature*, a term frequently used by Paul. Separation from the love of fellow believers, as well as exposure to dark forces, would hopefully lead the man to remorse and repentance—destroying the desires of his sinful nature. Paul wanted to eradicate what was fleshly in this man with the purpose of having the spiritual in him emerge. Both interpretations look toward the future judgment: that the man would be saved on the day of the Lord Jesus. The apostle wanted to protect him from a worse verdict when Christ would evaluate his life on judgment day.

Interestingly, Paul did not attack the guilty man or even name him. He rebuked, however, the Corinthians for allowing his immorality to go unchecked. He charged the church four times to remove the man from their fellowship (1 Cor. 5:2, 5, 7, 13). Their pride led to the failure to impose discipline. The purpose of this remedial, not punitive, action would help both the man (future judgment) and the church (removal of evil).

Although we should take action against cultural compromise in our church, we must conduct the discipline of expulsion in love for the redemptive purpose of motivating offenders to repent of sin. We should reserve such action for when persistent sin pollutes our whole church family and brings disgrace to our fellowship.

Understand the Effects of Cultural Compromise (5:6–8)

When one is ill, schools and employers urge the individual to stay at home to avoid the spread of the illness by infecting others. Paul knew the incestuous man's sin was infecting the entire congregation.

Paul described the Corinthians' boasting as "not good." The apostle used a baking metaphor to picture the effects of their cultural compromise. Just as a little leaven can spread throughout a batch of dough, so the bad influence of one person can lead other believers to sin. The Bible uses leaven as a symbol of evil and its contagious power. The church at Corinth needed to purge the old leaven, getting rid of it altogether. By expelling the offender—and their pride— the members of the Corinthian church would be like fresh, unleavened bread. In Christ, they had become new creations, a new lump (2 Cor. 5:17). Christ had removed their sin by his death, making them unleavened. The apostle wanted these believers to be pure in practice, to become what they actually were in Christ.

The apostle explained the background of his baking metaphor with the sentence, "For Christ our Passover also has been sacrificed." Before the Passover celebration, Jews searched through their homes to remove all leaven. The Passover meal included only unleavened bread. Women prepared the unleavened bread before the slaying of the Passover lamb. For believers, the Passover Lamb, Jesus, has already been sacrificed. The Corinthians were way behind in cleaning out the leaven in their midst.

Paul urged the Corinthians to celebrate the feast. He viewed the Christian life as an ongoing festival. Believers should celebrate not with sin, especially that of malice and wickedness, but with sincerity and truth. Malice and wickedness summarize every form of sin and belong to the old life. Sincerity and truth imply pure motives and actions that match commitment to Christ.

Cultural compromise by even one member of a church family can infect the entire congregation. Our holy God wants his holy temple to maintain moral purity. Let's become what we are in Christ—his holy people.

Do Not Tolerate Cultural Compromise (5:9–13)

We try to distance ourselves from a colleague who comes to work sneezing, coughing, feeling miserable, and complaining of aches and chills. Paul did not want the Corinthians to tolerate blatant sin in their midst.

The apostle addressed a misunderstanding caused by his previous, now lost, letter to the church at Corinth (see v. 9–10). Paul had instructed them to not associate with immoral believers. The Corinthians thought he had meant not to associate with all people. They would have to leave the world entirely to get away from those who were immoral or covetous (greedy), swindlers (those who steal by violence), or idolaters. And, not associating with non-Christians would hinder their efforts to make disciples.

Paul meant for them to not associate with someone who claimed to be a Christian if that individual was an immoral person, or covetous, or an idolater, or a reviler (one who verbally abused others), or a drunkard (often associated with idolatrous feasts), or a swindler. Though such a person professed Christianity, their lifestyle denied that claim. Paul urged the church not even to eat with such a person. Some interpreters believe this means the Corinthians were not to have intimate fellowship with the offender, breaking all social ties. Others contend that the man could no longer gather with the church for worship and teaching.

The apostle reminded the Corinthians that God judges those outside the church—nonbelievers. Believers, however, have the responsibility to confront sin within the church family. Paul ordered the church at Corinth to remove the wicked person from among them.

We should not tolerate those in our church whose lives are no different from those in the world and who do not intend to change. We need to confront them in love, both for their sakes and the sake of the church family.

Implications and Actions

This lesson makes me uncomfortable. It must make other believers uncomfortable also because I seldom see church discipline practiced. Perhaps we remember Jesus' words in Matthew 7:1, "Do not judge so that you will not be judged." However, Jesus was referring to hypocritical, self-righteous judging that excuses our own sins. Or, perhaps we wonder, *What's the point? If we discipline church members, they can go to another church.* Or, *What if they sue our congregation?*

Based on our lesson text, the Lord wants us to practice church discipline. It is a necessity, not an option. The best image for such discipline is a hospital emergency room—not a prison. We're trying to heal people. Discipline should have a therapeutic, restorative benefit for the person and the church family. We should never exercise this discipline over trivialities. Our church should take action against those who sin openly without remorse and whose sins affect the entire church family.

We should try to become this kind of church family: If we must exercise church discipline, we should do so in a manner in which those expelled would long to return, repent, and be welcomed back with love and forgiveness.

The Steps of Church Discipline

Church discipline purifies the church, restores sinning believers, deters church members from sin, maintains the credibility of the church's witness, and glorifies God. In Matthew 18:15–17, Jesus outlined several steps to take in exercising church discipline 1) Go to the sinning believer and confront the person in private with love, humility, and gentleness. If the individual listens and repents, you have won back that Christ follower. 2) If, however, the person refuses to listen to the private rebuke, return with one or two witnesses to confront the offender again. The witnesses confirm that sin was committed, the sinning church member rebuked, and whether the person repented. This protects everyone involved. 3) If the offender still has no change of heart, the witnesses should take the matter before the church. The church family should pray for, warn, and plead with the sinning believer to repent. 4) If the offender refuses to repent, the church must treat the person as an outsider, excluded from the fellowship. Jesus gave no time frame for this discipline.

Case Study

The Vacation Bible School leadership team met for a planning meeting. As they reviewed the list of people who had volunteered to help, Joy noticed Mary's name on the list. Joy asked the group, "Should we allow someone to serve as a worker who is living in sin? Is this the appropriate role model for our children?" Joy and many church members knew Mary had lived with her boyfriend for years. Their daughter came to children's activities at the church. Should the leaders allow Mary to serve in VBS? Why or why not?

Questions

1. Can you think of examples of churches who have condoned cultural compromise? What was their reasoning, and what were the results?

2. Why are church members reluctant to practice church discipline?

3. What danger does embracing cultural compromise pose for the church?

4. How did the Corinthians view sin? How does God view sin? How does your attitude toward sin affect your view of church discipline?

5. What consequences does your sin have on the life of your entire church?

6. Why is the Christian community intolerant with sinning unbelievers and tolerant with sinning believers? Should it be just the opposite? Why or why not?

lesson  4

Permissible or Beneficial?

MAIN IDEA

In exercising their freedom, Christ-followers should seek the good of others.

QUESTION TO EXPLORE

Is the exercise of my freedom a stumbling block to the faith of someone else?

STUDY AIM

To consider if the exercise of my freedom could cause other believers to stumble in their faith

QUICK READ

Paul instructed the Corinthians on the issue of meat sacrificed to idols. He encouraged them to seek the good of others and glorify God in exercising their freedom in Christ.

Introduction

During October, sermons of the pastor of the Hispanic mission of our church include an anti-Halloween emphasis. Ironically, my home church (which sponsors the mission) annually hosts a "Trunk or Treat" close to October 31. Hundreds of unchurched families attend this event, and we follow up with each family. We view this as an outreach opportunity.

Is the mission pastor right in insisting believers should not participate in Halloween because of its pagan origins, ghoulish costumes, and some sinful behavior? Or, is the sponsoring church right in viewing a Halloween-related activity as a gospel opportunity? Is Christian participation in Halloween permissible or beneficial?

When the Bible does not give a specific command, how should believers deal with "gray areas"? Paul's instructions to the Corinthians about eating meat offered to idols gives us contemporary guidance: in exercising our freedom, Christ-followers should seek the good of others.

1 Corinthians 8

[1] Now concerning things sacrificed to idols, we know that we all have knowledge. Knowledge makes arrogant, but love edifies. [2] If anyone supposes that he knows anything, he has not yet known as he ought to know; [3] but if anyone loves God, he is known by Him.

4 Therefore concerning the eating of things sacrificed to idols, we know that there is no such thing as an idol in the world, and that there is no God but one. 5 For even if there are so-called gods whether in heaven or on earth, as indeed there are many gods and many lords, 6 yet for us there is *but* one God, the Father, from whom are all things and we *exist* for Him; and one Lord, Jesus Christ, by whom are all things, and we *exist* through Him.

7 However not all men have this knowledge; but some, being accustomed to the idol until now, eat *food* as if it were sacrificed to an idol; and their conscience being weak is defiled. 8 But food will not commend us to God; we are neither the worse if we do not eat, nor the better if we do eat. 9 But take care that this liberty of yours does not somehow become a stumbling block to the weak. 10 For if someone sees you, who have knowledge, dining in an idol's temple, will not his conscience, if he is weak, be strengthened to eat things sacrificed to idols? 11 For through your knowledge he who is weak is ruined, the brother for whose sake Christ died. 12 And so, by sinning against the brethren and wounding their conscience when it is weak, you sin against Christ. 13 Therefore, if food causes my brother to stumble, I will never eat meat again, so that I will not cause my brother to stumble.

1 Corinthians 10:22–33

22 Or do we provoke the Lord to jealousy? We are not stronger than He, are we?

23 All things are lawful, but not all things are profitable. All things are lawful, but not all things edify. 24 Let no one

seek his own *good*, but that of his neighbor. **25** Eat anything that is sold in the meat market without asking questions for conscience' sake; **26** FOR THE EARTH IS THE LORD'S, AND ALL IT CONTAINS. **27** If one of the unbelievers invites you and you want to go, eat anything that is set before you without asking questions for conscience' sake. **28** But if anyone says to you, "This is meat sacrificed to idols," do not eat *it*, for the sake of the one who informed *you*, and for conscience' sake; **29** I mean not your own conscience, but the other *man's*; for why is my freedom judged by another's conscience? **30** If I partake with thankfulness, why am I slandered concerning that for which I give thanks?

31 Whether, then, you eat or drink or whatever you do, do all to the glory of God. **32** Give no offense either to Jews or to Greeks or to the church of God; **33** just as I also please all men in all things, not seeking my own profit but the *profit* of the many, so that they may be saved.

Freedom Should Build Up (8:1–6)

During my sophomore year of college, two friends and I had dinner with the faculty sponsor of our Christian organization. Imagine our teetotaler shock when this teacher ordered a beer, took a sip, and declared, "There's nothing better than a cold beer!" Exercising her freedom in Christ confused me. Paul addressed the Corinthians about their confusion over whether believers should eat meat offered to idols.

The words "Now concerning" indicate Paul was answering a question the Corinthians raised in their letter to him.

This concern related to three issues: eating meat sacrificed to idols in a pagan temple, buying this meat in the marketplace, and eating such meat in a private setting. [See sidebar "Meat Offered to Idols."] Paul emphasized that believers should never give the impression they were worshiping an idol, or that Christians could worship both God and other deities. Most pagans in Corinth worshipped many gods and goddesses. Christians must not follow this practice.

Some Corinthians flaunted their "knowledge." They knew idols or the deities they represented did not exist. They were free to eat food offered on a pagan altar. The Apostle Paul affirmed that knowledge can make one "arrogant," conceited, and proud—indifferent to others' needs. In contrast, he taught that "love edifies." Love strengthens others—and the church. Paul warned that people who think they know something still have a lot to learn. A relationship with God is more important than knowledge, and God knows those who love him.

Paul agreed that no such thing as an idol exists in the world. Pagan deities were nonexistent. The traditional gods the pagans worshipped or the lords of the mystery religions were only "so-called gods." Thus, eating food offered to idols was not wrong in itself. Food was morally neutral.

The apostle affirmed monotheism by stating, "there is but one God." He described God as "the Father," the Creator, the One for whom "we exist." Believers should live for God. They exist for his purposes. Paul described "one Lord, Jesus

Christ," as the agent of Creation and the One through whom we came into being. Christians are new creations in Christ.

Paul began his discussion on eating idol-meat by emphasizing love—not knowledge. He wanted the Corinthians to understand that love limits freedom. Those who paraded their knowledge were hurting believers and tearing down the church. The apostle corrected how they exercised their freedom. Christian liberty, like love, builds up.

In those neutral areas of decision-making, do your choices build up fellow believers, or do your actions hurt and confuse them?

Freedom Should Put Others First (8:7–13)

In June 2006, Ben Roethlisberger, the Pittsburgh Steelers' quarterback, was in a motorcycle accident requiring surgery for facial injuries. The athlete chose not to wear a helmet. Exercising his freedom put Roethlisberger's life at risk and impacted his teammates. Paul insisted that the Corinthians put the interests of others before their own, even if it meant limiting their freedom.

Corinthian believers who had come from a pagan background found it difficult to break old patterns of thinking. Throughout their lives, they had believed idols represented real gods. They had eaten meals sacrificed to idols, believing they were honoring these gods. Consequently, when they saw other Christians eating such meat, they viewed them as worshiping idols. Their "conscience" (moral compass) was "weak." They could not distinguish between sin and something morally neutral. Eating idol-meat made them feel "defiled" because they believed they were doing something wrong.

Paul knew that food had nothing to do with a believer's relationship to God. It did not matter what food they ate. All food, including idol-food, was neutral. The Corinthians' "liberty" (right) to eat meat used in pagan sacrifice, however, might become a "stumbling block" to those with a weak conscience. Some Corinthians believed they had the right to act as they pleased. However, their actions (done in freedom) might hinder the faith of those who had misgivings about this food. It might lead them to sin, including compromise with idolatry.

Those with knowledge understood that it was acceptable to eat anything, so they dined "in an idol's temple." However, if someone with a weak conscience witnessed them eating in such a place, they might feel strengthened to eat idol-meat also—even if they thought it wrong. Those professing knowledge would have "ruined" or destroyed the weak brother or sister for whom Christ died. Interpreters differ on the meaning of the word *ruined*. Some contend it refers to weakening the faith of believers, preventing their spiritual growth. Others suggest it means causing others to sin while some believe *ruined* refers to eternal, final destruction by those who fell back into idolatry.

Paul declared these freedom-acting Christians were "sinning against" fellow believers. They also wounded Christians whose consciences were "weak," thus causing them to do things they thought were wrong. Even more seriously, sinning against other believers meant sinning "against Christ." Freedom is not the only criterion in deciding actions. Love has priority.

Paul declared he would "never eat meat again" if it caused a fellow Christian "to stumble." Paul considered the interests of others as more important than his own rights. He wanted the church at Corinth to do the same.

Exercising our liberty in Christ is not sinning. We sin, however, when we use our freedom at the expense of fellow believers. We should be willing to make any sacrifice to help others mature as Christ-followers.

Will you put others first?

Freedom Should Glorify God (10:22–33)

When the herdsmen of Abram and Lot argued about pastureland for their flocks, Abram decided he and his nephew should separate. Although Abram was the family patriarch, he set aside his rights and allowed Lot to choose the land he wanted first. Abram's actions glorified God (Genesis 13.) Paul wanted the Corinthians to make decisions that glorified God.

Finally, Paul forbade eating meals in pagan temples. Those meals signified fellowship with deities whose idols represent the world of demons. Believers should not participate in any function openly related to idolatry (1 Cor. 10:14–21). God is a jealous God. He does not share his honor. Association with idol worship by attending feasts at pagan temples would "provoke the Lord to jealousy." Believers are not stronger than God.

Paul quoted a slogan perhaps used by himself or the Corinthians: "All things are lawful." This meant, "We have the right to do anything we choose!" The apostle reminded them, however, that "not all things are profitable or edify." Eating idol-meat in a pagan temple was not useful or constructive. The apostle gave a principle to guide believers' decisions: "Let no one seek his own good, but that of his neighbor." Believers should put the interests of others above their own—both fellow Christians and unbelievers. Love for others should determine their choices.

Paul provided practical advice for Christians living in a society filled with idolaters and markets flooded with meat sacrificed to idols. First, the Corinthians could eat any meat purchased in the market. He encouraged them not to ask questions about the meat to keep their consciences clear. They wouldn't know which meat had come from an altar, but food was morally neutral.

By quoting Psalm 24:1, a Jewish blessing at mealtimes, the apostle declared everything created by God was good and belonged to him. Believers should consider meat purchased in the market as food provided by God's love and goodness. Idol-based food loses its nature outside of the pagan temple and the purpose of the idol-worshiper.

Second, if an unbeliever invited a believer home for dinner, Paul encouraged acceptance of the invitation and to "eat anything that is set before you without asking questions for conscience' sake." The apostle did not want believers to withdraw from family, friends, and colleagues. If Christians did not know the meat was idol-meat, they would not think they were doing something wrong by eating the meal. Their conscience—moral compass—would be clear. If anyone at the meal, however, identified the meat as sacrificed to idols, then the guest believers should not eat the meat. The person would think believers were participating in idol worship, compromising the Christian confession of the one true God.

Paul defended believers' freedom to eat any food, especially if they considered food a gift from God and had offered thanks for it. How could they be condemned or slandered for this? Christians should not fear what other people think of them.

Paul gave a final principle to guide the Corinthians. "Whether, then, you eat or drink or whatever you do, do all to the glory of God." Believers' actions should glorify God. They should live so they do not offend others—whether Jews, Greeks (Gentiles), or fellow believers. Paul used himself as an example: He thought of others first and what benefited them as opposed to doing what was best for himself. The salvation of other people motivated the apostle, not his rights. He encouraged the Corinthians to "Be imitators of me, just as I also am of Christ" (1 Cor. 11:1). By following

Paul's pattern and Christ's prime example, they would build up the church, put others first, and glorify God.

Which reflects your attitude? My freedom in Christ allows me to do anything I choose. Or, I will limit my freedom to bring others into a saving relationship with Christ and so glorify God.

Implications and Actions

Believers have freedom in Christ. Rules and lists of things to avoid no longer order our actions. Authentic freedom, however, puts God and others first. We must reflect carefully on how we exercise our freedom. Do we consider how our actions impact others, or do we hurry to gratify our desires without thinking? When we allow love to shape our actions, we may at times find our liberty restricted. Love limits our freedom. Are you willing to embrace that limitation?

As Christ-followers, we should imitate Jesus. He exercised his freedom by submitting to death on the cross, revealing the Father's great love for us. When we follow his example, we will not demand our rights—conforming to the "me-first" culture. Instead, we will deny ourselves. We will exercise our freedom motivated by love that builds others up, puts them first, and glorifies God in everything we do.

How are you exercising your freedom? Listen to Paul's words in Galatians 5:13. "My friends, you were chosen to be free. So don't use your freedom as an excuse to do anything you want. Use it as an opportunity to serve each other with love" (Contemporary English Version).

Meat Offered to Idols

Corinth's temples allowed people to worship numerous gods and goddesses. These pagan cults included sacrifices often followed by a banquet in honor of the deity to whom the sacrifice was made. In animal sacrifices, part of the meat burned on the altar was for the god; a part went to the worshiper, and some to the priest. Often the priest's portion ended up in the local meat market, along with banquet leftovers. Many temples had large dining rooms and served as restaurants. It was proper social etiquette to have a meal in the temple. People rented the temples' banquet rooms for weddings, birthdays, meetings, and other events. Social meals eaten in the temple, however, always had a religious element because the gods were honored at that site and thought to be present. Christians who participated in civic life would have been expected to attend festival sacrificial meals. Refusing to participate would affect believers' family and social relationships, networking, and advancement in society. Survival in the ancient world depended on these social connections.

How to Exercise Christian Freedom

Before you exercise your freedom in Christ, particularly in morally neutral areas, evaluate your choices by asking yourself the following questions:

- Am I demanding my rights or acting in love?
- Am I causing other believers to do something they think is wrong?
- Am I helping my witness for Christ and bringing others into a saving relationship with him?
- Am I making a choice that is good and helpful for others?
- Am I thinking only of my interests, or am I considering the interests and needs of others?
- Am I glorifying God?

Questions

1. What issues in the church today revolve around whether specific behaviors are permissible or beneficial?

2. Why should we have to sacrifice our freedom for others?

3. How would you define the term *stumbling block*? When do you think you have been a stumbling block to fellow believers? to non-Christians?

4. What activities are you biblically free to participate in that you may need to give up for the sake of your Christian brothers and sisters? Do you love the body of Christ enough to surrender your rights?

5. How can you balance sensitivity to fellow believers with the need to guard yourself against those who intentionally or unintentionally turn Christianity into legalistic rules and regulations?

6. When have you wounded the conscience of a fellow believer? How is this sinning against Christ?

lesson 5

Gifted for the Common Good

MAIN IDEA

Spiritual gifts are given to believers to build up the body of Christ.

QUESTION TO EXPLORE

Have you identified, and are you using your spiritual gift(s)?

STUDY AIM

To discover and use my spiritual gift(s) in the church

QUICK READ

God has given the members of his church a wide variety of spiritual gifts to be used under his direction for the common good of the entire church.

Introduction

I have been attending a Baptist church most of my life, but for many years I had no idea that church was anything more than a weekly meeting where you learned about God. What was God's purpose in creating the church? Was church attendance just to be a go-and-sit encounter? Was it the place where one could learn to sing? What is the church supposed to be, and what is to be the role of the members?

During my years of college, I began to realize that the church is the body of Christ and that every member is to be an active and functioning part of the church. It is an organization where things are systematized and organized to carry out the mission of God through the ministries of that church. But even more importantly, the church is to be a living, active, functioning organism, described in 1 Corinthians 12 as the body of Christ. Why is it called the body of Christ? What is the difference between an organism and an organization? How is our church the body of Christ?

What is a spiritual gift? What are the spiritual gifts? Why do we have them? What is the purpose of a spiritual gift? We will discover answers to these questions in this lesson.

1 Corinthians 12:4–31

4 Now there are varieties of gifts, but the same Spirit. **5** And there are varieties of ministries, and the same Lord. **6** There are varieties of effects, but the same God who works all things in all *persons*. **7** But to each one is given the manifestation of the Spirit for the common good.**8** For to one is given the word of wisdom through the Spirit, and to another the word of knowledge according to the same Spirit; **9** to another faith by the same Spirit, and to another gifts of healing by the one Spirit, **10** and to another the effecting of miracles, and to another prophecy, and to another the distinguishing of spirits, to another *various* kinds of tongues, and to another the interpretation of tongues. **11** But one and the same Spirit works all these things, distributing to each one individually just as He wills.

12 For even as the body is one and *yet* has many members, and all the members of the body, though they are many, are one body, so also is Christ. **13** For by one Spirit we were all baptized into one body, whether Jews or Greeks, whether slaves or free, and we were all made to drink of one Spirit.

14 For the body is not one member, but many. **15** If the foot says, "Because I am not a hand, I am not *a part* of the body," it is not for this reason any the less *a part* of the body. **16** And if the ear says, "Because I am not an eye, I am not *a part* of the body," it is not for this reason any the less *a part* of the body. **17** If the whole body were an eye, where would the hearing be? If the whole were hearing, where would the sense of smell be? **18** But now God has placed the members, each one of them, in the body, just as He desired. **19** If they were all one member, where would the body be? **20** But now there are many members, but one body. **21** And the eye cannot say to the hand, "I have no need of you"; or again the head to the feet, "I have no need of you." **22** On the contrary, it is much truer that the members of the body which seem to be weaker are necessary; **23** and those *members* of the body which we deem less honorable, on these we bestow more abundant honor, and our less presentable members become much more presentable, **24** whereas our more presentable members have no need *of it*. But God has *so* composed the body, giving more abundant honor to that *member* which lacked, **25** so that there may be no division in the body, but *that* the members may have the same care for one another. **26** And if one member suffers, all the members suffer with it; if *one* member is honored, all the members rejoice with it.

27 Now you are Christ's body, and individually members of it. **28** And God has appointed in the church, first apostles, second prophets, third teachers, then miracles, then gifts of healings, helps, administrations, *various* kinds of tongues. **29** All are not apostles, are they? All are not prophets, are they? All are not teachers, are they? All are not *workers of* miracles, are they? **30** All do not have gifts of healings, do they? All do not speak with tongues, do they? All do not interpret, do they? **31** But earnestly desire the greater gifts.

And I show you a still more excellent way.

The Giver of Spiritual Gifts (12:4–11)

Paul made clear that God is the giver of all spiritual gifts. A gift, by its nature, is given by the generosity of the giver. A gift is not something earned; it is something given without merit.

In verses 4–7, the focus is on the origin of the gifts. The word "gifts" in verse 4 comes from the Greek word usually translated *grace*. This translation helps stress that the gifts are bestowed as an act of divine favor, and given to people unworthy of them. No person should assume his or her gift is more important than another's. The proud Corinthian believers boasted in their gifts but failed to realize that the gifts conveyed neediness, rather than self-competency.

These verses describe the gifts as varied. Three times Paul said, "There are varieties of gifts" be they gifts, ministries, or effects. The word translated "varieties" could be translated as *various, different kinds of,* or *different.* So, there are many kinds of spiritual gifts, but God is always the gift-giver (12:4–5).

There are varieties of gifts (spiritual skills), an assortment of ministries (serving methods), and variations of effects (effect-causing activities), but the same God is the activator of these gifts in all people. The gifts and the gifted people are instruments God uses to accomplish his purposes.

Paul concluded that each believer is given manifestations of the Spirit for the common good or benefit (v. 7). God—in all his fullness as the Holy Spirit, Son, and Heavenly Father—is involved in giving the gifts we receive and in providing the power that works through the gifts. Each believer receives at least one spiritual gift. The gifts are not to be used for self-elevation but to benefit the church body.

We read in verse 11 that the Spirit is at work in giving us our gifts and in the use of our gifts. It is God who distributes the gifts. When I was in college, I had friends who spoke in tongues, and while they respected my faith and knowledge of the Bible, they questioned my faith since I did not speak in tongues. Their concern for those of us who did not have their gift came across as pressure to get the gift. However, the precise teaching of Scripture is that there are many gifts, and everyone does not share any particular gift. Verse 11 states that God decides who gets what gift. It is not for us to seek something that God has not given to us. God gives the spiritual gifts to his followers for a reason or purpose.

Pray and ask God to reveal the spiritual gifts he has given to you and how he desires you to use those gifts for the common good and benefit of the church. It may be helpful to ask other believers who know you well to note spiritual gifts they see active in your life. It is often surprising to have several people, independent of each other, affirm a gift.

The Variety of Spiritual Gifts (12:4–11; 29–31)

God is a complex being, and he gives a wide range of gifts for the benefit of the church. The variety reveals the diversity and multi-faceted nature of God, as well as the diverse makeup of the church. Different people comprise the church, moving together in Spirit-orchestrated efficiency.

Why are there an array of gifts in any particular church? Let me give a practical illustration that may help answer that question. Why does a golf bag contain multiple clubs? A full bag may include two drivers, two fairway woods, six irons, a pitching wedge, a sand wedge, a ball-recovery scoop, a rescue club, and a putter.

Each club is different. It may have a different angle on the hitting edge, be a different weight or size, or be more open or closed as to how it will strike the ball. Good golfers use different clubs given the need for distance, loft, or backspin on the ball. When approaching the green, the golfer wants the ball to have height and backspin, so that when it hits the green, the ball loses momentum and stays on the green. You wouldn't use a putter to drive off the tee, and you wouldn't use a pitching wedge to putt on the green. (Unless you broke your putter during the round!)

The need for multiple golf clubs is a metaphor for the variety of gifts required by a church. God has multiple ministries and assignments for each church to carry out, different types of gifts are required at various times. But all the gifts are given to the church for a purpose, as are the ones needed in particular situations. We all have gifts and roles to fulfill which God uses to benefit the church and ministry.

Corinth was a town full of sailors from a variety of countries and language groups. If they were to hear the gospel, someone needed to be gifted by God to speak the gospel via a language they had personally never learned. It became a problem when members gifted to speak in other languages used their gift as a sign of spiritual superiority, thereby misusing the gift. Gifts have a proper time and manner in which to be used, and God is the one who determines the time and place.

Using Spiritual Gifts in the Body of Christ (12:12–27)

Paul made clear that every church is to function as the body of Christ (12:12). Members are to manifest Christ living among their community. As individuals, we are to bear witness to the reality of Jesus, who is alive in us. As a group of diverse people with diverse gifts, each church is directed and empowered by the Lord to vibrantly reveal Christ in daily living, serving, and impacting the people in a city and the world.

In 1 Peter 4:10, we learn that each believer has received a special gift that should be employed wisely by serving one another. The church is like a human body, comprised of many individual parts, each with its particular function and responsibility, but all working together with the other components to empower the body to function as it should. Likewise, when members of the church body work together, the body of Christ performs as it should.

As the church, Christ lives in us, animates us, gifts us, and empowers us to coordinate and work together to present our living Savior to a world who has not seen or known him. The human body has many parts: eyes, ears, nose, mouth, tongue, lungs, heart, feet, hands, as well as less obvious ones. All the parts play vital roles. Many must function all the time (such as the heart and lungs), while others (hands or feet) are engaged as needed.

However, all the parts of the body of Christ are to continually connect, for at any particular moment one may be the crucial element required to carry out a task. Church members who are rarely attached to the body are not being what God created them to be. We each need the church, just as your finger always needs the rest of your body. We need the church and what it contributes to life. The church needs each of us, and the gifts and abilities we add. Together, we can reveal the beauty of Christ far better than any one of us could do alone.

Implications and Actions

Spiritual gifts are given to each of us to help the church function as Christ moving in our community. To do this, we must remain connected to the rest of the church, stay alert to God's instructions, and use our gifts as he gives us opportunity for the common good of the church. We are to care for one another, treating each member as invaluable because each is a living part of Christ's body. God designed the church to be a living organism, not just an organization.

We need to use our gifts in conjunction with the other body parts, under Christ's leadership, to accomplish what God desires to do through the church. The body functions all day every day, not just on Sunday.

You are a member of the body of Christ (12:12). What has God gifted you to do in helping your church be the active living presence of Jesus moving about in your community, helping people experience his love and power?

Spiritual Gifts and How to Use Them

Some of the spiritual gifts appear in 1 Corinthians 12:8–10; others in Romans 12:6–8 and Ephesians 4:11–13. Here are a few ways spiritual gifts are lived out in daily life (from 1 Cor. 12:8–10).

- Word of wisdom (ability to give practical spiritual advice)—v. 8

- Word of knowledge (helpful scriptural information)—v. 9

- Miraculous faith (exemplifying belief during difficult circumstances)—v. 9

- Gifts of healing (God healing through believers)—v. 9

- The effecting of miracles (miraculous power released through believers)—v. 10

- Prophecy (powerful preaching—both foretelling and forthtelling)—v.10

- Distinguishing of spirits (ability to discern difference between God's Spirit and evil ones)—v. 10

- Speaking in various kinds of unlearned languages—v. 10

- Understanding unlearned languages—v. 10

The Gift of Various Languages

Regarding the gift of various languages mentioned in 1 Corinthians 12:10 (see also 12:30; 14:2–4, 10, 12, 18–19), there are differing views as to whether the use of the word *tongues* denotes spiritual endowments of unlearned human languages or speaking in a type of heavenly language.

In this verse, the word *tongues* is the Greek word *glossolalia*, which can mean the physical tongue, but when used as a plural, it usually refers to *languages*. The speaking in tongues that occurred at Pentecost (Acts 2:4–6) referred to believers empowered to speak in unlearned human languages, which visitors heard in their various dialects. The Corinthian context here could refer to this or could be a so-called "prayer language" of ecstatic praise to God.

Either way, Paul made clear in 1 Corinthians 14 that speaking in tongues/languages which were not understandable by all should not be practiced in the church group. Gifts used in the church services should be gifts that build up, enrich, and benefit the entire church (cf. 14:2–4, 10–12, and 18–19).

Questions

1. Think of a time when, because of an injury, you couldn't use an eye, arm, hand, or leg for a week or more. How did the loss of the use of that body part affect your daily functioning? Share your insights with the group.

2. When members of the church only attend or participate periodically, how does their absence affect the healthy functioning of the church as the body of Christ?

3. List the spiritual gifts you believe God has given to you.

4. What are some areas where your spiritual gifts could help your church to function efficiently?

5. Why should church members work together?

6. What spiritual gifts do you see present in a fellow class member that perhaps he or she does not recognize? Take a couple of minutes to share your observations with that individual.

lesson  6

The Most Excellent Way

MAIN IDEA

Love infuses life with meaning.

QUESTION TO EXPLORE

How do you define the word *love*?

STUDY AIM

To evaluate my expressions of love by its biblical description

QUICK READ

God's love is to be the motive for what we do, the makeup of who we are, and the way we do everything. Love never fails and it never ends.

Introduction

While in college I had the opportunity to attend a multi-day conference entitled "Becoming a Lover." What college guy wouldn't be interested in that subject? Dr. Paul Cedar led the event, and those three days changed my life. Today's lesson is the heart of what it means to be a Christian and love one another.

Jesus taught that the world would know we are his disciples by the way we love one another (John 13:33–34), and that love in our lives indicates we live in God and God lives in us (1 John 4:16).

Love is among the most prevalent subjects in the world of literature and songs. So, how would you define love? Is love a feeling? Do mushy, gushy words symbolize it? Is it philosophical ideas and ideals? If Christians are commanded to love each other, and we don't know what love is, then how can we fulfill Jesus' command?

Are you ready for an adventure? Are you eager to discover a new dimension of living and loving? In this lesson we'll consider the biblical definition of love.

1 Corinthians 13

1 If I speak with the tongues of men and of angels, but do not have love, I have become a noisy gong or a clanging cymbal. **2** If I have *the gift of* prophecy, and know all mysteries and all knowledge; and if I have all faith, so as to remove mountains, but do not have love, I am nothing.[3] And if I give all my possessions to feed *the poor,* and if I surrender my body to be burned, but do not have love, it profits me nothing.

[4] Love is patient, love is kind *and* is not jealous; love does not brag *and* is not arrogant, [5] does not act unbecomingly; it does not seek its own, is not provoked, does not take into account a wrong *suffered,* [6] does not rejoice in unrighteousness, but rejoices with the truth; [7] bears all things, believes all things, hopes all things, endures all things.

[8] Love never fails; but if *there are gifts of* prophecy, they will be done away; if *there are* tongues, they will cease; if *there is* knowledge, it will be done away. [9] For we know in part and we prophesy in part; [10] but when the perfect comes, the partial will be done away. [11] When I was a child, I used to speak like a child, think like a child, reason like a child; when I became a man, I did away with childish things. [12] For now we see in a mirror dimly, but then face to face; now I know in part, but then I will know fully just as I also have been fully known. [13] But now faith, hope, love, abide these three; but the greatest of these is love.

Love as Motivation (13:1–3)

Love should be the reason we do things and should guide how we do them. Love motivates Christians (cf. 13:1). Eloquent words and sermons that are not driven by love are like a dentist's drill squealing in your mouth. Sweet words from a mean person hit the listener like fingernails dragged down a chalkboard. Proclaiming heavenly things with self-ish motives is like the dissonant feedback from multiple cymbals playing concurrently but to a differing beat.

Hitler was an effective orator, but his words were motivated by self-aggrandizement and hatred, not by love. He destroyed most of Europe and decimated ethnic people groups to fulfill his dream of a new world order with him at the head. Human skills and gifts used by destructive individuals produce destruction.

Many individuals in the Corinthian church had powerful gifts, but they used them for self-promotion instead of the good of the whole church. Good gifts used with corrupt motivations produce caustic results.

Those who spoke in tongues in Corinth presumed their gift was the ultimate, and that they spoke for God. They did not use the gift in love to build up others. Instead, they were competing to be the "most spiritual person in the church." Instead of serving with humility, they trampled others.

Possessing the gifts of prophesy, wisdom, or knowledge but not using them in love produces no lasting spiritual benefits (13:2). Love should motivate believers as they preach, counsel, or advise others. The self-motivated use of gifts tears down others to build up self. In contrast, love sets ego aside to build up others.

Having extraordinary faith—even being able to have a mountain plucked up and thrown into the sea—is dangerous if not motivated by, and exercised in love. Power corrupts. Human nature typically abuses power. Without love, one might be able to throw mountains into the sea, but take no thought of those destroyed in the process. Love asks, *How many people live on that mountain? Can they swim? Will they die from the impact of the mountain crashing into the sea?* Love asks, *Will the splashdown create a tidal wave, and who will that harm?* Individuals who use power without love or no thought of their impact on others, are destructive and dangerous. Without love guiding remarkable powers, the resultant actions are useless.

If not done in love, acts of charity (13:3) and even martyrdom accomplish nothing. Love makes something valuable.

Love motivated everything Jesus did. Love for us propelled him to leave heaven and take on flesh, live among us, be mocked, abused, mistreated, and brutally crucified. Love for us helped him set his face toward Jerusalem, knowing that suffering and death on a cross awaited him. Love for God, and us, motivated him not to quit when he asked God in the garden at Gethsemane if it were possible to avoid the brutal suffering which awaited him.

Love for God and others must motivate our actions. We love because we choose to love. We are doing it because God loves us; therefore, we should love God in the same manner (cf. 1 John 4:11; John 13:34–35). We are to love others the way Jesus loves us.

Love as Our Standard (13:4–8)

Love is practical and tangible, therefore love's activity is observable and measurable. In verses 4–8, Paul presented the superlative characteristics of God's love. We are to demonstrate love in our character and actions. Our motives, nature, and deeds should manifest God's love. Love is present tense; love is active, not passive.

We see in verse 4 that love is patient, gentle, and useful in dealing with others. It is not possessive nor jealous but trusts others. Love doesn't focus or brag on itself but builds up others.

From verse 5, we learn that love is mature and steady rather than unpredictable. It is polite and not rude. Love does not insist on getting its way but considers the needs of others. Love doesn't let others provoke it to inappropriate action. It doesn't hold grudges but instead forgives and releases others from offenses.

God's love isn't happy when evil instigates havoc but delights when truth and righteousness take center stage (13:6). Verse 7 capsulizes love's pragmatic, enduring character. Paul explained that love is tenacious in holding up under pressure and is steadfast in believing God will prevail in the end. Love optimistically maintains a hope-filled disposition in all circumstances and keeps moving forward against dire circumstances.

Love as Christian Character in Motion (13:9–12)

At the close of Paul's discussion of spiritual gifts in 1 Corinthians 12:31, he said, "But earnestly desire the greater gifts. And I show you a still more excellent way." The Corinthian believers were infatuated with spiritual gifts, but Paul stressed love, something superior to individual gifts. Spiritual gifts without love are like drills without a power source. They are fruitless.

The love explained in 1 Corinthians 13 is God's love (translating the Greek word *agape*). It is a love that flows out of God's nature. In 1 John 4:7–12, we discover God is love, and when God comes to live within us, he fills us with himself and thus his love. A Christian's nature becomes infused with God's love, which becomes a significant part of a Christian's makeup. Further, John said that love is not that we loved God, but that God first loved us and gave Jesus as the appeasement for our sins. God's love is sacrificial, and it takes the initiative in building good relationships, even with unlovely people (cf. Romans 5:6–10). So, God's love is revealed by the Christian nature in motion.

Love recognizes and affirms value in others. We were hopeless sinners, lost in despair, without God and devoid of hope (Romans 5). God loved the world and sent Jesus to die for us. His love made us valuable. Love does that. A person who has been woefully neglected can suddenly bloom under the touch and encouragement of God's love.

God's love is volitional; it is an act of the will. It is not merit-based, does not respond to stimulation or manipulation, and is not duty-bound. God's love is a choice. He does not love us because we are skillful, enjoyable, or beautiful. God loves us because he chooses to love us. It is a love that chooses to love another, regardless of reciprocity. Love is an act of our will.

God's love operates in the present tense. Love is not something of the past; nor some "pie in-the-sky" hope. Love is present and active now. Love is superior, above all else. Love is beyond feelings, beyond pain, beyond difficulty. Love endures, it never comes to an end, and is ever-present. God is love. God never fails. God is eternal and lives within the believer. His love in and through us embodies those characteristics as well.

Implications and Actions

Today's Scripture should meld deeply into the soul of the believer. God is love, and the love depicted here is the kind of nature, characteristics, and relationships that God desires to see developed in each of our lives. God brings these traits to us when he comes to live within us, but we need to actively cultivate and increase this love in all aspects of our lives.

Love should be who we are as people. It should also become the reason we think what we think and do what we do. Love should be the way we relate to one another. Our quality and quantity of love should continually grow in all areas of our lives like the enlarging concentric circles that radiate from a stone thrown into a pond, growing larger as they go farther out from the original point of contact. We should read 1 Corinthians 13 often to guide us to discover new ways to express love. The passage can serve as our end-of-day benchmark (especially verses 4–8) as we each replace the word *love* with our name, read the chapter again, and evaluate our day's behavior.

Evaluate Your Love

Utilizing the traits listed in 1 Corinthians 13:4–7a, evaluate God's love in your character, motivations, and actions.

- Am I patient? Am I gentle and useful to others?
- Do I jealously try to control others, or do I trust them to make decisions?
- Do I seek my agenda above all, or put others first?
- Do I brag more about my accomplishments than about those of others?
- Am I quick-tempered? Do I do kind things for those who provoke me?
- When upset, am I childish and rude, or mature and polite?
- Do I keep a list of wrongs done to me and seek retaliation, or do I forgive my offenders?
- Do I stand against injustices done to others and advocate treating everyone properly?

- Do I carry difficult loads when necessary? Do I endure harsh treatment? Do I hope the best for others? Do I get up and go again when knocked down? Do I give up on love or keep loving against all odds?

Case Study: Love Doesn't Insist on Its Own Way

A church has two competing factions regarding the appropriate music style to use in worship. One camp insists on hymns. The other side asserts the church must shift from hymns and organs to praise music led by a band. Each faction is adamant about why their style of music should be dominant.

How could love as described in 1 Corinthians 13 be applied to this problem? What aspects of love are missing from the scenario? What aspects of love could lead to an amicable solution?

Questions

1. Why did Paul state that love is the most excellent way, a gift better than all the others?

2. Why is demonstrating love often forgotten or neglected among Christians today?

3. Why do we need to always show love to others while we can do so?

4. How might our lives be enriched if love motivated everything we do in life? Why does the use of a spiritual gift need to be motivated by love? What happens when it is? What happens when it is not? Give an example.

5. Why did Jesus say the world would recognize us as his disciples by the love in our lives? Why didn't Jesus say that the world would know we are his disciples by our wisdom or peace? Why is love the litmus test?

6. How would your life change if you:

- Read 1 Corinthians 13:4–7 each morning to remind you of the kind of person God expects you to be?

- Set out to demonstrate a trait of love to specific people each day?

- Evaluate your behavior each night by reading the passage to see if you lived out love during the day?

lesson  7

Live with Resurrection Hope

MAIN IDEA

We can live with confident hope because of Jesus' resurrection.

QUESTION TO EXPLORE

How do the facts of the resurrection and Christ's return give you confident hope?

STUDY AIM

To live with confident hope because of Jesus' resurrection

QUICK READ

The resurrection of Jesus gives us hope that God's power can defeat anything we face in life, and certainty that Jesus will raise us from the dead in the future.

Introduction

One of the ministries of Texas Baptists is BOUNCE Student Disaster Recovery.[1] This ministry mobilizes junior high and high school students to serve communities which have suffered natural disasters. This past summer, BOUNCE teams worked in cities along the Texas Gulf Coast that were hit by Hurricane Harvey.

The BOUNCE motto is: "Restoring Hope, Rebuilding Communities, Reflecting Christ." The hope BOUNCE offers to residents who have lived through catastrophic events is rooted in the Scripture found in this lesson. Paul reminds us in 1 Corinthians 15 that because of Jesus' resurrection, we can all live with confident hope, regardless of the storms in our lives.

1 Corinthians 15:3–20, 35–44, 50–57

3 For I delivered to you as of first importance what I also received, that Christ died for our sins according to the Scriptures, 4 and that He was buried, and that He was raised on the third day according to the Scriptures, 5 and that He appeared to Cephas, then to the twelve. 6 After that He appeared to more than five hundred brethren at one time, most of whom remain until now, but some have fallen asleep; 7 then He appeared to James, then to all the apostles; 8 and last of all, as to one untimely born, He appeared to me also. 9 For I am the least of the apostles, and not fit to be called an

apostle, because I persecuted the church of God. ¹⁰ But by the grace of God I am what I am, and His grace toward me did not prove vain; but I labored even more than all of them, yet not I, but the grace of God with me. ¹¹ Whether then *it was* I or they, so we preach and so you believed.

¹² Now if Christ is preached, that He has been raised from the dead, how do some among you say that there is no resurrection of the dead? ¹³ But if there is no resurrection of the dead, not even Christ has been raised;¹⁴ and if Christ has not been raised, then our preaching is vain, your faith also is vain. ¹⁵ Moreover we are even found *to be* false witnesses of God, because we testified against God that He raised Christ, whom He did not raise, if in fact the dead are not raised. ¹⁶ For if the dead are not raised, not even Christ has been raised; ¹⁷ and if Christ has not been raised, your faith is worthless; you are still in your sins. ¹⁸ Then those also who have fallen asleep in Christ have perished. ¹⁹ If we have hoped in Christ in this life only, we are of all men most to be pitied.

²⁰ But now Christ has been raised from the dead, the first fruits of those who are asleep.

• • • • • • • • • • • • • • • • •

³⁵ But someone will say, "How are the dead raised? And with what kind of body do they come?" ³⁶ You fool! That which you sow does not come to life unless it dies; ³⁷ and that which you sow, you do not sow the body which is to be, but a bare grain, perhaps of wheat or of something else. ³⁸ But God gives it a body just as He wished, and to each of the seeds a body of its own. ³⁹ All flesh is not the same flesh, but there is one *flesh* of men, and another flesh of beasts, and another flesh of birds, and another of fish. ⁴⁰ There are also heavenly

bodies and earthly bodies, but the glory of the heavenly is one, and the *glory* of the earthly is another. **41** There is one glory of the sun, and another glory of the moon, and another glory of the stars; for star differs from star in glory.

42 So also is the resurrection of the dead. It is sown a perishable *body*, it is raised an imperishable *body*; **43** it is sown in dishonor, it is raised in glory; it is sown in weakness, it is raised in power; **44** it is sown a natural body, it is raised a spiritual body. If there is a natural body, there is also a spiritual *body*.

• • • • • • • • • • • • • • • • •

50 Now I say this, brethren, that flesh and blood cannot inherit the kingdom of God; nor does the perishable inherit the imperishable.**51** Behold, I tell you a mystery; we will not all sleep, but we will all be changed, **52** in a moment, in the twinkling of an eye, at the last trumpet; for the trumpet will sound, and the dead will be raised imperishable, and we will be changed. **53** For this perishable must put on the imperishable, and this mortal must put on immortality. **54** But when this perishable will have put on the imperishable, and this mortal will have put on immortality, then will come about the saying that is written, "DEATH IS SWALLOWED UP IN VICTORY. **55** O DEATH, WHERE IS YOUR VICTORY? O DEATH, WHERE IS YOUR STING?" **56** The sting of death is sin, and the power of sin is the law; **57** but thanks be to God, who gives us the victory through our Lord Jesus Christ.

The Meaning of Christ's Resurrection (15:3–20)

Apparently, there was confusion in the Corinthian church surrounding aspects of Jesus' resurrection from the dead and its implications for the believers in Corinth. To address these misunderstandings, Paul began with the reality of Jesus' resurrection, then moved to the meaning of it for the life and faith of believers. We base our present and future hope of resurrection on the certainty that Christ died for our sins and God raised him from the dead. To live confidently today, we must stand on the faithfulness that God raised Jesus from the dead in the past.

The death, burial, and resurrection of Jesus are paramount in our understanding of the meaning and power of the Christian faith. Paul claimed that these things are of first importance (v. 3) in our faith, namely that Christ died for our sins.

Since the time of Adam and Eve, humanity has had a problem that must be solved, namely the issue of our sin. Since those first sins against God, humans have had the propensity to use free will to sin against God. The Bible states that all have sinned and fall short of the glory of God (cf. Romans 3:23), coupled with the penalty for our sin being our death (Rom. 6:23).

However, the gift of God is eternal life in Christ Jesus our Lord. God's justice declared that the soul who sinned would die. God's love and grace proclaimed, "He [Jesus] who knew no sin, became sin [took our sins upon himself] for us,

so that we could become the righteousness of God in Him."
(2 Corinthians 5:21). Christ died for our sins; he paid our
penalty in full. When we commit ourselves to Jesus, our
sins are transferred to him on the cross and buried in his
grave with him. Without the shedding of blood [the penalty of death], there is no remission of sin. Christ died for us
to cancel our sins, forgive them, and set us free from their
power.

God resurrected Jesus for our justification (cf. Rom. 4:24).
He raised Jesus from the dead to prove:

- Jesus was sent from God and told the truth. God would
  not raise up a liar.
- Jesus' sacrifice was successful and accepted.
- God forgave us. Romans 4:23 explains that we have
  become justified in Christ, forgiven and clean and
  righteous in the sight of God.
- Jesus defeated sin and death.
- In Jesus, we are changed to live forever with God, even
  though we die physically (John 5:21–29).

All the things Jesus accomplished through dying for us and
rising from the dead are fulfillments of the Scriptures, i.e.,
fulfillments of God's divine will and purpose to give us a
living hope (1 Peter 1:3–5).

The resurrection of Jesus is historical fact, and a list of
many of the people who interacted with the risen Christ
subsists (cf. 1 Cor. 15:5–9). More than 500 eyewitnesses
saw Jesus and interacted with him after he rose from the

dead. This corroboration is foundational in infusing hope in each of us so that we can confidently face anything because God is faithful and all powerful. Jesus told the disciples he was going to die but would rise from the dead and appear to his disciples. He said, ". . . because I live, you will live also" (John 14:19).

Jesus rose on the third day (1 Cor. 15:4) as he said he would. We now have the assured hope that a day is coming when God will raise us from the dead. Life after death for us is as sure as the fact that Jesus defeated death.

Our Resurrection Bodies (15:35–49)

Paul next turned to the theme of our resurrection bodies. He posed two questions: How are the dead raised, and what will our bodies be like? (cf. v. 35). To answer these questions, Paul used several illustrations to help us understand how this works. The overarching word-picture comes from farming or gardening.

Paul began by stating that in sowing a seed, God gives each seed a body (v. 38). So, our resurrected bodies will possess unique characteristics, as well as shared traits. God designed heavenly bodies for the environments of space and human bodies for the earth's biosphere. In verses 42–49, Paul explained that the mortal body has the image of the human (Adam), and a heavenly body will bear the image of the heavenly resurrected Christ. Just as we now have earthly bodies, we will later have heavenly ones suited to that environment.

On a humorous note, for those of us who are overweight, this is a good definition of hope: As Christians, we will eventually all have heavenly bodies! Eugene Peterson captured the pre-resurrection and post-resurrection body differences in his translation of 1 Corinthians 15:42–44 in *The Message* (see sidebar).

The bottom line? We go into the ground unimpressive, but God will raise us up as extraordinary. Our bodies, frail and weak when buried, will rise full of strength and life. Our physical bodies are buried as perishable, but our souls rise as imperishable. We die in dishonor only to rise clothed in honor and glory. The physical life came first, but the spiritual life will surpass it. As sure as we have physical bodies for our earthly existence, we know we will have spiritual bodies for life in the presence of God (see 1 Cor. 15:40; 42–44; 45–49). We can't totally comprehend what we will look like or what our new bodies will be capable of, but we do have some hints by evaluating what Jesus' resurrected body could do.

The Mystery of the Resurrection (15:50–57)

In these verses, Paul explained the mystery of the resurrection which occurs at the sound of the last trumpet, when Christ returns (15:52; 1 Thessalonians 4:13–18). To understand, we must realize the biblical meaning of the Greek word "mystery" meant *to explain something that formerly was not understood, but which is now understood,* hence a solved puzzle. In English, the word "mystery" implies an unsolved puzzle, or a yet to be discovered secret. So, what is this solved mystery?

In verse 51 Paul said, "Behold, I tell you a mystery: we shall not all sleep, but we shall all be changed." In Old Testament Judaism, even up until the resurrection of Jesus, the afterlife was unknown. The Hebrew word *Sheol*, which meant "the shadowy unknown" or "the place of shadows," was often used to reference the afterlife. This theological perspective was the core controversial divide between the Pharisees, who believed there was a life after death (a resurrection), but were unsure about the kind of life it would be, and the Sadducees, who didn't believe in life after death.

Jesus proved there is life after death by rising from the dead and interacting with people for more than forty days in his resurrected body. So, Paul was essentially saying that something we once failed to understand, we now comprehend: There is a resurrection of the dead. There is life after death with a different genre of body. And all believers will experience it. As believers, we will undergo a metamorphosis. God will change our human bodies. They will have some of the same nature as before, but will also have newfound quality and dimension.

A day is coming when all believers who have died prior to Jesus' return will hear his voice and be resurrected, and at the same time the believers who are still alive when Christ returns, will all be raised up, and changed on the way up. What were our earthly bodies will be changed to heavenly ones (1 Cor. 15:51–57, see also 1 Thess. 4:15–17). All believers will be changed together to meet the Lord and forever be with him.

On that day, the transformation will happen instantaneously. Mortal bodies will rise as imperishable, what was weak will be raised in power, what was natural will be raised spiritual (1 Cor. 15:42–44). When the perishable has put on the imperishable, and the mortal has put on immortality, then the victory over sin and death will be complete (15:53–57).

Implications and Actions

The death of Jesus made our ultimate redemption and transformation possible. Jesus' shed blood was the sacrifice required to fulfill God's righteous requirement for sin through the penalty of his death. Perfect Jesus died in our place to cleanse us from sin. The resurrection broke the power of sin and death. Neither sin nor death can keep a believer separated from the love, power, and presence of God. God raised Jesus and revealed him to many witnesses so that we would understand that his resurrection is true.

In Jesus we are forgiven, so when Jesus comes to live in us via the Holy Spirit, we have eternal life and will never perish. Jesus gives us the capability to defeat temptation and sin. When we die physically, we know God will raise us with glorified, heavenly bodies in which sin will never exist. Therefore, we live in hope. God has won, and we merely await him bringing us across the finish line into heaven. Thank God for his incomparable gift (2 Cor. 9:15).

1 Corinthians 15:42–44 from *The Message* (MSG)[2]

"This image of planting a dead seed and raising a live plant is a mere sketch at best, but perhaps it will help in approaching the mystery of the resurrection body—but only if you keep in mind that when we're raised, we're raised for good, alive forever! The corpse that's planted is no beauty, but when it's raised, it's glorious. Put in the ground weak, it comes up powerful. The seed sown is natural; the seed grown is supernatural—same seed, same body, but what a difference from when it goes down in physical mortality to when it is raised up in spiritual immortality!"

Understanding Hope

Hope is a word with a variety of uses. "I hope it won't rain tomorrow." "I hope next year will be prosperous for us." "I hope the chemotherapy will destroy my cancer cells."

Hope is an optimistic attitude of looking toward a good outcome for something that threatens to affect our lives today. Biblical hope adds other elements to this definition. It is not just wishful thinking. A hope-filled Christian stands firmly on the demonstrated faithfulness of God in the past to bring about his purposes in the future. Based on God's faithfulness, hope allows us to face all kinds of uncertainty in the present and keep moving forward past obstacles and naysayers toward the future when what God has promised will be revealed. Biblical hope is possessing the virtue of optimism coupled with faith in a trustworthy God. Hope-filled believers live expectantly, waiting for God's future intervention.

Questions

1. Why is the fact Jesus rose from the dead important to you?

2. Describe something unusual that has happened to you that others may have difficulty believing. Do the doubts of others negate your belief that the event occurred? Why or why not?

3. How does the fact Jesus died and rose from the dead affect your perspective on the death of a loved one? How does it affect you when contemplating your death?

4. Why are many today not excited to realize Jesus rose from the dead? Should it be an awe-producing event just as much today as it was in the first century?

5. What is the most exciting thing you look forward to doing after you receive your heavenly body?

6. How does the resurrection of Jesus give you hope to live the Christian life each day?

NOTES

1. http://texasbaptists.org/ministries/missions/disaster-recovery/bounce (Accessed 5/26/18).

2. Scripture quotations marked MSG are taken from *THE MESSAGE*, copyright © 1993, 1994, 1995, 1996, 2000, 2001, 2002 by Eugene H. Peterson. Used by permission of NavPress. All rights reserved. Represented by Tyndale House Publishers, Inc.

Introducing 2 Corinthians

Refute, Restore, and Raise Hope

"Refute, Restore, and Raise Hope" serves as an outline to describe the Book of 2 Corinthians. Ongoing issues in the church at Corinth, and in Paul's relationship with the church, prompted additional correspondence. Lesson eight shows how when we receive comfort from God, it can overflow to others in need. Lesson nine provides counsel for healing broken relationships and lesson ten offers advice for overcoming the challenges of ministry. Lesson eleven reveals how we can give and receive criticism in the proper manner, while lesson twelve focuses on integrity as a key for solving disputes. Lesson thirteen reminds us that God's grace is sufficient to meet all our needs.

2 CORINTHIANS: REFUTE, RESTORE, AND RAISE HOPE

lesson  8

Serving Through Suffering

MAIN IDEA

God comforts us in our troubles, so our comfort can overflow to others in need.

QUESTION TO EXPLORE

How can God's comfort in our lives overflow and provide hope for others?

STUDY AIM

To allow the comfort God provides me to overflow and bring hope to others

QUICK READ

Paul understood suffering for the gospel allowed God's power to flow through him to bless and encourage others.

Introduction

In 1917, my great-grandmother penned the following words as part of a twenty-page letter to her loved ones in New York, describing her experiences and surroundings in Colorado, where she and her husband had recently begun ministering.

> *Have you ever heard of a barbeque? We never had either. The people were gathered in groups the same as any ordinary picnic, but they had dug a great trench, perhaps four feet by twelve feet in which they built a fire. When it had burned down mostly to live coals, they put a rack over it, placing great chunks of beef which had been killed for the occasion. On beyond the beef, which the tenders turned now and again with pitchforks, which they stuck again into the ground, were two or three wash-tubs full of coffee steaming hot.*

In our culture of texts, emails, emojis, and tweets, to receive a newsy letter from a loved one is unusual. I envision Paul, like my great-grandmother, writing with deep emotion to those he loved. Paul had a more critical agenda than passing along news of his surroundings. The apostle wrote from Macedonia (probably Philippi) in A.D. 54 or 55 to instruct the church regarding pressing matters, including how believers can have hope and comfort during suffering.

2 Corinthians 1:1–11

1 Paul, an apostle of Christ Jesus by the will of God, and Timothy *our* brother,

To the church of God which is at Corinth with all the saints who are throughout Achaia:

2 Grace to you and peace from God our Father and the Lord Jesus Christ.

3 Blessed *be* the God and Father of our Lord Jesus Christ, the Father of mercies and God of all comfort, **4** who comforts us in all our affliction so that we will be able to comfort those who are in any affliction with the comfort with which we ourselves are comforted by God. **5** For just as the sufferings of Christ are ours in abundance, so also our comfort is abundant through Christ. **6** But if we are afflicted, it is for your comfort and salvation; or if we are comforted, it is for your comfort, which is effective in the patient enduring of the same sufferings which we also suffer; **7** and our hope for you is firmly grounded, knowing that as you are sharers of our sufferings, so also you are *sharers* of our comfort.

8 For we do not want you to be unaware, brethren, of our affliction which came *to us* in Asia, that we were burdened excessively, beyond our strength, so that we despaired even of life; **9** indeed, we had the sentence of death within ourselves so that we would not trust in ourselves, but in God who raises the dead; **10** who delivered us from so great a *peril of* death, and will deliver *us*, He on whom we have set our hope. And He will yet deliver us, **11** you also joining in helping us through your prayers, so that thanks may be given by many persons on our behalf for the favor bestowed on us through *the prayers of* many.

From Problems to Purpose (1:1–4)

Opening salutations in first-century correspondence generally followed a standard pattern: the sender to a recipient, a greeting, then an expression of thanks. Writing with Timothy,[1] his apprentice, Paul expanded on this, identifying himself as "an apostle of Christ Jesus by the will of God" (1:1), because the Corinthians had questioned his authority. Paul knew well the history and character of the Corinthian church, and succumbing to the influence of charismatic charlatans was a weakness.[2] In this case, false apostles divided the church as they preached their diluted versions of truth, demanded payment from people, cast aspersions on Paul's teachings, and denied his legitimacy as an apostle because he wasn't one of the original Twelve (see sidebar "An Apostle of Jesus Christ").

Paul's letter was to the "church of God." The word *church* (Gr. *ekklesia*) described a gathering of citizens to voice their thoughts, but Paul distinguished them as people who gather to hear God's voice.[3] He called them "saints" (i.e., holy ones set apart from evil) among those "throughout Achaia," the local region which included Athens and Cenchrea, where there were known converts. Although this letter wasn't necessarily intended to travel throughout the area (in contrast to the message for the Galatians), Paul was reminding the Corinthians of the bigger picture. Nearby believers could testify to his apostleship! Furthermore, their diversion from truth might impact other churches in the region negatively.

It's almost amusing that Paul described them as saints considering how much turmoil the church experienced. But Paul, like God, saw not only who these believers were in their sin, but who they would become with Christ's redeeming, ever-reshaping work accomplished in their lives.

Paul's traditional greeting, "grace" and "peace," sought for them God's unmerited care and well-being borne of fulfillment, which stemmed from a right relationship with God through Christ (1:2). However, his word of thanks wasn't to (or for) the Corinthians. Instead, Paul blessed God for providing him comfort in affliction and deliverance from adversity (1:3–4). In this respect, 2 Corinthians differs from the apostle's other known correspondence because it begins with an unusual focus on God's work through him, instead of what God was doing in the Corinthian believers. In fact, the absence of thanksgiving for them may indicate the rift between Paul and the church. Unfortunately, the Corinthians, under the leadership of false apostles (and like many believers today), thought a Spirit-filled person lived a trial-free life filled with the miraculous. Paul's struggles, they thought, revealed God's absence in his life.

Paul certainly knew affliction well. In 2 Corinthians 11:23–33, he listed numerous sufferings (imprisonments, lashings, stonings, shipwrecks, sleepless nights, hunger and thirst, and so forth). But early in this epistle he expressed why his sufferings were necessary, so he could "comfort those who are in any affliction with the comfort with which we ourselves are comforted by God . . . [the] Father of mercies and God of all comfort" (1:3–4).

Twenty-first century believers define comfort as freedom from displeasure, but the English word *comfort* derives from the Latin *confortis* meaning "brave together" or "strong with," which is the idea Paul employed.[4] It's not necessarily a tranquil, contented feeling, but rather consolation from God that boosts resolve, buoys fortitude, brightens spirits, builds endurance, and brings assurance, even against all logic. God comforted Paul at the beginning of his faith journey, promising a divine purpose for his life (Acts 22:14–21). In 2 Corinthians 12:9, God assured Paul his grace was sufficient even in the midst of an issue that grieved Paul deeply. God delivered Paul from peril numerous times.[5]

From Calamity to Comfort (1:5–7)

Paul used two different root words for external and internal adversity: "affliction" (Gr. *thlipsis* from the root meaning *to press*) and "suffering" (Gr. *pathema* from the root meaning *emotional experience* resulting from misfortune, physical pain, or death). Paul likened his sufferings to Christ's (1:5) because he was suffering so others might be saved, not because he pursued his own agenda or self-glorification. Christ, not regarding "equality with God a thing to be grasped" (Philippians 2:5), suffered, died, and rose again so we might gain salvation's abundant and comprehensive peace for eternity. Christ's suffering was the platform by which "God demonstrate[d] his own love toward us" (Romans 5:8).

Paul's suffering was the platform upon which God revealed his power and furthered the gospel (cf. Phil. 1:12–14). Tradition says during his Roman imprisonment, Paul's guards were constantly replaced because they kept coming to Christ! In fact, Jewish persecution led Paul to remain in Corinth eighteen months wherein he preached the gospel and established the church (2 Cor. 1:6; Acts 18:1–11).

Even if the Corinthians weren't suffering when Paul wrote 2 Corinthians, he knew they might someday. Or he may have been contrasting his struggles with their peace, suggesting their lives weren't much different than the pagans around them. To be clear, Paul didn't glorify suffering as a sign of spiritual maturity or imply there were various levels of suffering to be achieved. Furthermore, Paul didn't try to explain away his suffering, focus on it, or stoically endure it;[6] instead, his suffering drove him to trust God alone, enduring through God's strength, not his own. Those who helplessly stood by watching Paul's adversity, witnessed God's faithfulness, and were then equipped to patiently endure sufferings.

Fear, resentment, and bitterness aren't necessary, either, since Jesus told his disciples to expect persecution (John 15:20; 16:33). Paul even appreciated the opportunity to know Christ better by sharing in his sufferings (cf. Phil. 3:10). He didn't view difficulty as an oddity in a Christian's journey and neither should we. Because humans desire self-management and Satan has temporary control in this world, we should expect to suffer because both clash with absolute surrender to God. However, believers have "firmly grounded" hope (meaning *with planted feet*) as we endure our adversities with patient expectation, assured of God's profound comfort (2 Cor.1:7) and knowing his eternal purposes will be enacted (Rom. 8:28).

God longs to grow his children to trust him in all circumstances. To the degree we experience suffering, we experience God's comfort. Grace is made manifest in affliction. In fact, God's reassurance not only matched Paul's suffering but exceeded it enough that an overflow existed to spill onto others. Although humans can't divinely deliver others, we can be God's conduit through which he encourages them with our words as we meet their needs and offer grace and a listening ear.

From Despair to Deliverance (1:8–11)

Paul pointed to a specific, recent experience on the west coast of Asia Minor as an object lesson in which God's comfort came in the form of deliverance from presumed death (1:8ff; see sidebar "What the 1:8 Affliction in Asia May Have Been"). Paul rarely addressed his trials in his epistles, so this incident must have been heavy on his heart, particularly to appear so early in his letter. The apostle did not specifically list the affliction (i.e., *thlipsis*) because his focus was on God's deliverance, but it burdened him so heavily it was beyond his strength to endure. He and those with him doubted they would survive, and likely feared their demise would hinder the gospel's continued spread to the Gentiles. The uncommon word *exaporethenai* ("despaired") implied Paul had no exit; his life hung by a thread. Nevertheless, he found when he trusted not in himself, "but in God who raises the dead"[7] (1:9; cf. Daniel 3:13–18; Hebrews 11:17–19, 35), the depth of God's comfort and deliverance matched the gravity of his trouble.

God's faithfulness in this instance assured Paul of future deliverance, as well (2 Cor. 1:10). This hope (not wishful thinking, but secure, confident conviction, cf. Hebrews 11:1), engenders a sense of triumph surpassing circumstance and time. In fact, Paul emphasized this saying, God "delivered us . . . will deliver us . . . will yet deliver us." He assumed there would be more tribulations (and deliverance) to come!

For Paul, intercessory prayer was the key. Paul usually mentioned his prayers for the churches at the beginning of his letters, requesting prayers for himself near the end. However, in 2 Corinthians 1:11, he asked them to join "in helping us through your prayers." He vulnerably confessed he wasn't a spiritual superhero. Inviting the Corinthians to pray for him proved he not only needed the God who delivered him, but he needed them, his fellow brothers and sisters in Christ. In turn, they reciprocally needed him as a divinely inspired leader. Essentially, Paul was asking the Corinthians to give thanks for his suffering, which was what they thought disqualified him as an apostle!

However, sharing crises and retelling them deepens human connections, and Paul's intent in sharing this incident in Asia was strategic. He knew God would work in them while they prayed for him. The prayers of the Corinthians would prompt appreciation and respect, they would no longer disparage his tribulations, and praying would help them recognize Paul's humility and frailty.

In addition, they would acknowledge that Paul's purpose was to honor God (not glorify himself), resulting in thanksgiving for God's work in his life. These changes would mark their trust in Paul's apostleship. Furthermore, praying for him was a deliberate and concrete step toward reconciliation because praying for others connects hearts in inexplicable ways. The resulting unity would bring glory to God.

Implications and Actions

We don't have to seek out suffering or welcome it, but we don't have to shield ourselves or flee from it either because God (the only source for genuine, enduring comfort) is strong enough to encourage us through it or deliver us from it. Unfortunately, many of us run at the first sign of difficulty. Our perspective of God usually affects our tenacity. If we see him as strong, but not good, we won't trust his compassion to see us through. If we see him as good, but not strong, we won't trust his ability to undergird us.

We live in a fallen world, so bad things happen to good people, but God longs to comfort his children

(Isaiah 51:12; 66:13; 2 Cor. 7:6). In fact, Romans 8:31–39 promises that nothing can separate us from God's love in Christ. As he comforts us, we have the privilege of comforting others because he gives an overflowing surplus. He doesn't just intend for us to feel better, he intends for us to "bear one another's burdens" (Gal. 6:2). Focusing only on ourselves limits the eternal, far-reaching effects of God's comfort in our lives, and when we do comfort others, God is glorified.

An Apostle of Jesus Christ

Modern church life has no equivalent to an apostle since that age ended with the disciple John's death on Patmos. Thus, many of us don't understand the role's gravity in the first century. By definition, an apostle is an emissary authorized and commissioned to carry out a personal mission on someone else's behalf.[8] Apostles were ascribed preeminent authority in churches because their gospel proclamations were firsthand accounts. The church viewed them as prophetic mediators between God and themselves, making their instructions regarding church practices virtually absolute.

Thus, in his letter to the Corinthians (2 Cor. 1:1) Paul designated himself as an apostle to defend himself and remind them why they should heed his instruction. He was not attempting to repair his reputation; he was asserting his divinely commissioned authority to speak into their lives because if they rejected him, they denied the message God sent through him. Paul didn't choose this vocation. Instead, the risen Christ personally appointed and authorized him with the responsibility of spreading the gospel to all Gentile regions (Acts 9:1–22; Gal. 1:15–16).

What the 1:8 Affliction May Have Been

- The riot in Ephesus (Acts 19:23–20:1). After denouncing idolatry, Paul and his companions were roughed up and nearly hanged.
- Exposure to beasts in Ephesus (1 Corinthians 15:32).
- A near-fatal illness. However, Paul customarily called persecution "affliction." Moreover, he said "we." Unless those with him were also fatally sick, this theory seems unlikely.
- Imprisonment or potential execution in a civil court not recorded in Acts.
- Intense opposition from Jews, which perhaps began in Asia and continued in Jerusalem (Acts 21:27).

Paul's lack of detail encourages discretion in reports of persecution to be confident God gets the glory, not human self-will to survive.

Questions

1. Are you tempted to assume adversity is related to sin? Would you have doubted Paul's apostleship when you observed the struggles he faced? Why or why not?

2. Describe a time of tribulation or persecution when you sensed God's comfort. How did you know it was God's presence? Why do you have hope in times of despair? How does that hope manifest itself in your daily life?

3. Describe a time when God used you to comfort another in difficulty or relate a time when someone else's suffering was "for your comfort" (1:6). Have you expressed appropriate gratitude to that individual?

4. How faithfully do you remember to pray for those with whom you have conflict? Have you ever avoided praying for someone because you didn't want to see the relationship reconciled? What happened?

5. Do you think Western culture Christianity understands the meaning of afflictions and sufferings in the sense Paul meant them? Why or why not? Are you tempted to label inconveniences (e.g. disrespect or lack of material goods) as afflictions? How does Paul's perspective on suffering reshape your thinking about your difficulties?

6. Spend some time in prayer for persecuted church members across the world. God knows who they are, but you can pray more specifically for them by visiting www.icommittopray.com (Voice of the Martyrs) or

www.opendoorsusa.org/take-action/pray/ (Open Doors). Pray also for the missionaries your church supports through mission offerings.

7. Have you ever suffered for your faith? If so, what happened?

8. How has God comforted you in the midst of suffering?

9. Have you ever been able to use painful experiences from your past to offer comfort to others?

10. What is the purpose of our sufferings?

NOTES

1. Apparently, Timothy visited Corinth to instruct the church (1 Corinthians. 4:17; 16:10) and returned with a troublesome report, prompting this letter. Perhaps Paul mentioned him to endorse Timothy's teaching since his own was in question. He didn't claim Timothy had apostleship, but he certainly wanted him trusted as a faithful brother in Christ, who, by virtue of being named, ascribed his witness of Paul as an apostle and his agreement to the words Paul wrote. Furthermore, mentioning Timothy proved Paul wasn't a maverick with his own ideas and opinions, but a cooperative member in church leadership.

2. This problem wasn't unique to Corinth (cf. Rom. 16:17–18; Gal. 1:6–9; Phil. 1:15–17; Colossians 2:8; 2 Timothy 3:1–7; 4:1–5; Titus 1:10–11).

3. A.T. Robertson, *Word Pictures in the New Testament,* Volume IV, The Epistles of Paul (Grand Rapids: Baker Book House, 1931), 51.

4. The Greek root *parakleo* Paul uses is the same Jesus used to describe the Holy Spirit *paraklete* in John 14:16.

5. Cf. 2 Cor. 7:6; 11:32–33; Acts 16:22–26; 23:11 to list a few.

6. David E. Garland, "2 Corinthians," *The New American Commentary,* Vol. 29 (Nashville, Tennessee: Broadman & Holman Publishers, 1999), 57.

7. This phrase came from Jewish liturgy. The tenses he used indicate a permanent character trait or attribute, not a one-time or unusual occurrence or ability. Paul was contrasting God Almighty with Greek/Roman gods. In fact, most first-century pagans eschewed the idea of resurrection, since Zeus allegedly killed Asklepios with a thunderbolt for disrupting the natural order by learning to restore the dead to life. http://www.theoi.com/Ouranios/Asklepios.html. (Accessed 12/19/17).

8. Scott J. Hafemann, "2 Corinthians," *NIV Application Commentary* (Grand Rapids, MI: Zondervan Press, 2000), 43. Electronic text hypertexted and prepared by OakTree Software, Inc. Version 1.7.

lesson 9

Tough Love to Stand the Test

MAIN IDEA

A forgiving spirit and honest communication can heal broken relationships.

QUESTION TO EXPLORE

How can we heal broken relationships?

STUDY AIM

To extend a forgiving spirit and honest communication to others so broken relationships can be healed

QUICK READ

Paul took proactive steps to heal his broken relationship with the Corinthian believers because unity in the body of Christ was a greater priority than his pride or reputation.

Introduction

In the New Testament, authors use the word *boast* forty-four times. Twenty-eight of those uses are in Paul's letters to the Corinthians; twenty in 2 Corinthians alone. Why all the references to boasting? Pride was apparently an issue in first-century Corinth for Christ-followers and non-believers.

Situated on a coast, Corinth was a city at a crossroads. (It was the gateway to the Peloponnese isthmus and part of the portage route from Lechaeum to Cenchrea.). Money and ideas flowed freely in Corinth. Famous for its manufacture of bronzeware, it became Greece's principal southern commercial center and served as the capital of the senatorial province of Achaia, as well as the seat of the region's proconsul.

Corinth lauded itself on the Isthmian games, an athletic competition occurring every other year, second only to the Olympics in prominence. A diverse city, it consisted of wealthy families, slaves, veterans, Gentiles, and Jews. The city also hosted a new class of people akin to our modern-day middle class: freedmen who were no longer slaves and had the opportunity for increased socioeconomic status. All these people groups exercised a spirit of independent thinking in a melting pot of philosophies, lifestyles, and religions.

Prostitution was a significant money-making industry in Corinth, supported by various pagan religions which used sexual intercourse as worship rites. Entrenched in Hellenistic culture, the Corinthians espoused what would later become known as Gnosticism, the belief that all material or physical existence is substandard or evil compared to the immaterial or spiritual. Thus, they were prone to intellectual pride about their knowledge, many philosophies, and spiritual experiences.[1] Unfortunately, this attitude bled into the church, often creating boasting, competition, disunity, and openness to false doctrine presented by charismatic new leaders. (See 1 Corinthians 1:10; 3:3; 6:6–7 and Lesson 8, where Paul addressed false apostles.)

Fundamentally, pride lay at the heart of the issues Paul addressed in his second epistle to the Corinthian church, egotism that damaged relationships. Since church unity was vital to Paul, he wrote to his beloved friends to remind them that a forgiving spirit and honest communication can heal broken connections between believers.

2 Corinthians 1:12–24

12 For our proud confidence is this: the testimony of our conscience, that in holiness and godly sincerity, not in fleshly wisdom but in the grace of God, we have conducted ourselves in the world, and especially toward you. **13** For we write nothing else to you than what you read and understand, and I hope you will understand until the end; **14** just as you also partially did understand us, that we are your reason to be proud as you also are ours, in the day of our Lord Jesus.

15 In this confidence I intended at first to come to you, so that you might twice receive a blessing; **16** that is, to pass your way into Macedonia, and again from Macedonia to come to you, and by you to be helped on my journey to Judea. **17** Therefore, I was not vacillating when I intended to do this, was I? Or what I purpose, do I purpose according to the flesh, so that with me there will be yes, yes and no, no *at the same time*? **18** But as God is faithful, our word to you is not yes and no. **19** For the Son of God, Christ Jesus, who was preached among you by us—by me and Silvanus and Timothy—was not yes and no, but is yes in Him. **20** For as many as are the promises of God, in Him they are yes; therefore also through Him is our Amen to the glory of God through us. **21** Now He who establishes us with you in Christ and anointed us is God, **22** who also sealed us and gave *us* the Spirit in our hearts as a pledge.

23 But I call God as witness to my soul, that to spare you I did not come again to Corinth. **24** Not that we lord it over your faith, but are workers with you for your joy; for in your faith you are standing firm.

2 Corinthians 2:1–11

1 But I determined this for my own sake, that I would not come to you in sorrow again. **2** For if I cause you sorrow, who then makes me glad but the one whom I made sorrowful? **3** This is the very thing I wrote you, so that when I came, I would not have sorrow from those who ought to make me rejoice; having confidence in you all that my joy would be *the joy* of you all. **4** For out of much affliction and anguish of heart I wrote to you with many tears; not so that you would be made sorrowful, but that you might know the love which I have especially for you.

5 But if any has caused sorrow, he has caused sorrow not to me, but in some degree—in order not to say too much—to all of you. **6** Sufficient for such a one is this punishment which *was inflicted* by the majority,**7** so that on the contrary you should rather forgive and comfort *him*, otherwise such a one might be overwhelmed by excessive sorrow.**8** Wherefore I urge you to reaffirm *your* love for him. **9** For to this end also I wrote, so that I might put you to the test, whether you are obedient in all things. **10** But one whom you forgive anything, I *forgive* also; for indeed what I have forgiven, if I have forgiven anything, *I did it* for your sakes in the presence of Christ, **11** so that no advantage would be taken of us by Satan, for we are not ignorant of his schemes.

A Clear Conscience (1:12–2:4)

Writing to a proud people, Paul expressed pride and joy in his integrity. He wasn't glorifying himself; he just wanted them to understand his conscience was clear. Because of the Holy Spirit's transformative work in his life and his calling as an apostle, Paul had conducted himself toward the Corinthians with holiness, sincerity, wisdom, and grace (i.e., undeserved kindness birthed from love), not human understanding or behaviors (1:12). Though charged by the Corinthians of insincerity—they accused him of saying one thing but intending another (1:13)[2]—Paul defended his correspondence as guileless and straightforward. He posited that he did not rely on cunning words to impress or deceive them in his previous writings.

He wrote sincerely, expecting God's power to bring about successful results. Paul hoped the Corinthians would be proud of his integrity and God's work through him, just as he planned to celebrate God's work in their lives on Judgment Day when God will evaluate all motives and behaviors (1:14). Paul was confident God would exonerate him on that day, but he wanted the Corinthians to affirm his integrity based on his life's evidence. Doing so would reveal their acknowledgment of God's power at work through his weakness, as well as their level of spiritual maturity. Most importantly, it would rejoin their hearts to his, and he wouldn't have to fear the congregation's loss to apostasy.

In this poised state of integrity, Paul then explained a choice he made which some apparently misunderstood as hypocrisy. In 1 Corinthians 16:5–7, Paul announced he planned to visit the church "after I go through Macedonia." However, for reasons unclear to us, he determined it best to change those plans so he might visit them twice: on his way to and from Macedonia (2 Cor. 1:15–16). Unfortunately, it appears he executed neither plan as intended (see sidebar "A Change of Plans"), so Paul appeared fickle, and they questioned his integrity (2 Cor. 1:17).

The false apostles infiltrating the Corinthian church may have used his change of plans to publicly call into question his boldness, genuine concern for their well-being, and motives. (Was Paul defrauding or taking advantage of their generosity with the Jerusalem offering?)

To avoid being accused of acting impulsively ("according to the flesh"), Paul hoped to reclaim the Corinthians' trust in his character by assuring them the Spirit prompted his change of plans. God was his witness to the veracity of his word (1:18). Jesus, Paul reminded them—the Jesus he, Silvanus, and Timothy preached to them as a threefold testimony (see Deuteronomy 19:15)—was not inconsistent, having fulfilled God's promises and every Old Testament Messianic prophecy.

Likewise, Paul's intentions never changed, just his plans. Thus, in Jesus, the "Amen" (meaning "yes" or "so be it"), Paul asserted his integrity was intact to the glory of God (1:19–20). Parenthetically, he added they, too, had the privilege of standing firm with integrity because at salvation, God anointed and gave all believers the Holy Spirit who speaks only truth (John 14:17; 15:26; 16:13; 1 John 5:6). The Spirit serves as a guarantee for those in Christ that God "establishes" us (Gr. *bebaion*, a legal term of commitment and validity between a seller and purchaser). He sealed (i.e., labeled) us as his own, claiming us as rightfully belonging to him (2 Cor. 1:21–22).

Paul then returned to the issue at hand. He called God as a witness against his very life (inviting divine judgment if he were lying), that he postponed the intended second visit to avoid another painful one (1:23). He wasn't unstable or dishonest, nor did he fear their rejection or damage to his reputation. However, if he had returned, he would have felt compelled to deal with those rebelling against his apostolic authority, perhaps even leading the church to remove them for creating disunity among the believers (cf. 1 Cor. 5:13 and 2 Cor. 13:2–3).

The apostle knew such action would even more deeply damage already tenuous relationships. His restraint, therefore, demonstrated Christlike compassion. If he sought tyranny over them, he would have arrived heavy-handed and domineering (Gr. *kurieuomen*, "lord it over"). Instead, he knew he was called by God to work with and for their joy, to serve them faithfully, not merely vindicate his reputation when called into question. Paul could not and should not dominate over them. Their faith created their standing before God. Ultimately, they were subject to God and no one else, so they should stand firm in their faith (2 Cor. 1:24).

Although translations divide Paul's letter into a new chapter at this point, he continued to explain his change of plans. He canceled his return visit because he sought their mutual joy and well-being, not desiring to create more sadness in dealing with the unresolved issues on the same trip. Personally, he was already sad enough about the broken relationships. Why would he want to make sorrowful those who usually brought him such joy?

As fellow believers, Paul's delight related to their own (especially as they grew spiritually), and grief for them meant sorrow for himself (2 Cor. 2:1–3). So, from Ephesus, he wrote a tearful letter to them (one lost to history) that brought him "much affliction [i.e., oppression] and anguish [i.e., distress] of heart," but communicated the concern and deep, unconditional, self-sacrificing love he had for them (2:4). It was a difficult letter to write but one Paul had to script.

Although a few scholars suggest the letter was 1 Corinthians, most believe Paul penned it after 1 Corinthians and his sorrowful visit, but before 2 Corinthians, meaning he wrote at least three epistles. The letter, delivered by Titus, apparently included warnings and calls to repentance which led some of the Corinthians to restore their trust in Paul. Paul hoped this epistle would do the same, especially since he desired to revisit them (2 Cor. 12:14; 13:1) in an atmosphere of joy, peace, and unity. Paul was optimistic about their relationship's healing.

A Compassionate Plea (2:5–11)

At first glance, 2 Corinthians 2:5–11, seems unrelated to the previous part of Paul's letter. In addressing the issue of an offender, we see the church's doubts about Paul were evidently spurred on by this unnamed individual. He may have been living in some form of overt or rebellious sin, and therefore challenged Paul's authority during the visit because he didn't want to change his ways. Then, Paul's change of plans and subsequent absence prompted slander. After all, people caught in sinful behaviors often deflect attention from themselves by pointing out others' shortcomings.

There's a slight possibility this is the same incestuous individual mentioned in 1 Corinthians 5, whom the church had perhaps eventually expelled. Whatever he did, this man's behaviors damaged the church, and they'd taken action of some kind (2:5–6). However, he was evidently repentant, and Paul, like Christ, was more interested in restored relationships than personal vindication, punishment, or revenge. He challenged the Corinthians to "forgive and comfort him," and "reaffirm [their] love for him" to reconcile and reestablish him in their faith community (2:7–8). Although his greatest priority was the church's unity, Paul was still concerned for the man's mental and emotional well-being, not wanting him "overwhelmed by excessive sorrow."

With the discretion of his compassionate pastor's heart, Paul graciously and deliberately did not mention the offender's name, despite the unrest and disunity he'd caused. Just as he showed mercy to the Corinthians for grieving him, Paul challenged them to display the same compassion to this repentant soul. In so doing, they would offer the man a reminder of the assurance of God's forgiveness, and give Paul further evidence of their willingness to acknowledge his apostolic authority.

Paul's instruction in his previous letter concerning this man was a test of their obedience (2:9). He assured them Christ could testify he'd already forgiven the man. They were to follow his example (2:10), not only for the offender's sake but also to prevent Satan from inflicting further damage on the church or God's kingdom work. Paul knew Satan takes advantage of pride to exacerbate conflict in Christ's body. The enemy leads a Christian family member astray, then tricks the church into withholding genuine love, acceptance, and forgiveness by bearing grudges, exploiting moral failures, or exacting punitive punishment instead of restorative discipline (2:11). Tough love must root out these behaviors, correcting and preventing them.

Implications and Actions

When division occurs within Christ's body, it's important to remember our struggle isn't against other disciples; it's against the father of lies (Ephesians 6:12; John 8:44) who comes to steal, kill, and destroy (John 10:10). Jesus, however, came to give abundant life, and part of that abundance is a faith journey shared with other believers. Richness and encouragement are found in walking by faith together.

Unfortunately, because we all wrestle with pride, we sometimes fight with one another, resist leadership, and promote personal agendas. That's when we need someone to love us enough to express truth and biblical expectations, and erect guidelines or boundaries. Doing so is tough, even painful at times, but is necessary for mending relationships. Our unity expresses to the lost world what it means to be in Christ's family (John 13:35), and when we refuse to forgive, we essentially tell them Jesus withholds forgiveness, too, a lie Satan uses to push them farther from salvation.

Reconciliation begins with you and me. We must take the initiative. Paul didn't wait for the Corinthians to apologize. Instead, he optimistically took the first step, trusting God with the results. He couldn't force a change of behavior or opinions, but he expected God to transform and unite hearts. God still does.

A Change of Plans

Apparently, Paul's original route was to be: Ephesus to Macedonia to Corinth to Jerusalem. But before writing 2 Corinthians, he changed his plan to: Ephesus to Corinth to Macedonia to Corinth to Jerusalem. Perhaps this was to give the Corinthians a second opportunity to give to the Jerusalem offering he collected from all the churches and then invite Corinthian elders to accompany him in presenting it to the Jerusalem believers.

Instead, Timothy returned with disconcerting news about the Corinthians (1 Cor. 4:17; 16:10). Paul's actual itinerary became: Ephesus to Corinth (which became the "sorrowful visit" of 2:1 and changed his agenda) back to Ephesus, to Troas to Macedonia (from whence he wrote 2 Corinthians). The Corinth visit was painful due to accusations questioning Paul's apostolic authority and integrity. In fact, someone may have publicly confronted him. This lack of trust grieved Paul. Not because his reputation was on the line, but because if the church doubted his trustworthiness as God's messenger, they would question his messages from the Lord.

Practical Application Exercises

Option 1. Script a letter to someone with whom you have a strained relationship. Use Paul's letter as a model or excerpts from his message put into your own words.

Option 2. Several years ago, Maria's husband confessed to infidelity with a coworker who claims to be a believer. He was genuinely repentant, and Maria forgave him. From time to time, Maria still sees the coworker in their community. She recently wrote the woman a letter, stating she had forgiven her, but the contact was rebuffed. Although they were never friends, what biblical wisdom would you offer Maria about additional steps to take, if any, to mend the relationship? If none, why not?

Questions

1. Throughout today's passage, Paul explained his actions, not to vindicate himself, but to restore understanding and relationship. When you've been misunderstood, do you seek vindication or restored relationship? Do you struggle with defensiveness or feel confident in what you know to be true, regardless of others' opinions? How do you communicate with those with whom your relationship is strained?

2. Do you find you want to control others' opinions of you? What do you do to combat that temptation?

3. Confronting a difficult situation is painful, even when done in love (Ephesians 4:15). How willing are you to address a conflict head-on in a Christlike manner as Paul did? Can you relate a time when you had to do that or someone did that with you?

4. Do you find forgiveness easy to receive but difficult to offer; or perhaps easy to offer, but difficult to receive? Why?

5. Are you optimistic about finding healing in damaged relationships or do you presume things won't improve? Why? Have you ever felt like you responded in a Christlike manner to someone who offended you and found the relationship didn't improve, or they weren't trustworthy? What did you do about it?

6. Granted, the church is not to overlook or condone members' sinful behaviors, but neither can the body of Christ refuse reconciliation to a repentant believer. Describe your understanding of the church's responsibilities in such a situation and support your opinion with Scripture. What are the consequences of not taking disciplinary action, and what are the advantages to executing it? Include in your discussion the effects on church unity and Satan's schemes. Why is unity important?

7. When was the last time you experienced a strained relationship? What can you do to bring healing to the relationship?

8. How can you forgive others in spite of their criticism?

NOTES

1. Gerald F. Hawthorne, Ralph P. Martin, and Daniel G. Reid, Eds. *Dictionary of Paul and His Letters.* (Downers Grove: Intervarsity Press, 1993), 172–3.

2. They also accused him of hypocrisy because of the strong tone of his letters (they thought he was weak in person—see 2 Cor. 10:10), peddling the gospel for profit (although he'd taken no income from them—see 11:7–9), and not being an authentic apostle, mistakenly believing his suffering was evidence Paul was not inspired or called by God (2 Cor. 1:5–6; 11:21–33; Acts 9:15–16; 28:3–4; Romans 8:17).

lesson  10

Maintain an Eternal Perspective

MAIN IDEA

A focus on eternity provides us with confidence to face the challenges of ministry.

QUESTION TO EXPLORE

How can we overcome the challenges of ministry?

STUDY AIM

To understand how a focus on eternity can provide confidence to face ministry challenges

QUICK READ

An eternal perspective empowered and motivated Paul to endure struggles, difficulties, and persecutions so people could still receive ministry, and so God's kingdom could expand as he shared the gospel.

Introduction

Typically, I'm not a quitter. I most often see things through to their glorious (or bitter) end. It's my nature and personality. However, my second year of college, I quit on swimming. I needed a physical education credit (PE), so I opted to take a swimming class, looking forward to sprinting a few laps (which I typically enjoyed) and having fun splashing with friends. What I didn't count on was how serious the instructor was about actually swimming! He expected me to use particular forms and specific styles. My head, torso, arms, and legs had to conform to his prescribed technique to earn a passing grade. It was hard, and I dropped the class. I quit.

The problem wasn't the instructor. It was me. I wanted to have fun earning a PE credit; his goal was to make me an excellent swimmer. I didn't want to endure the correction or challenges and wasn't willing to commit the time and effort necessary for improvement. My focus and perspective weren't enough to see the class through to semester's end. I wimped out.

Ministry isn't for wimps either! Sure, there are gratifying and joyful moments. But ministry can be dirty, frightening, unstable, and disappointing. And then, there are the people. They're messy, fallible, unkind, hardheaded, ungrateful, opinionated, uncooperative, and unreliable.

Challenged as a true apostle (Lesson 8), doubted as a man of integrity, defamed by a disgruntled church member, and grieved by broken relationships (Lesson 9), Paul experienced ministry's highs and lows. Nevertheless, his purpose was ministering for God's glory and kingdom expansion, despite challenges and disappointments. As fellow believers, that's our calling too (Matthew 28:19–20). We may want to quit or wimp out. Sometimes the only way to endure is to look past circumstances and focus on the gospel's eternal goal. We may need to focus our perspective on the long-term to confidently pursue our God-given ministry assignments.

2 Corinthians 4

1 Therefore, since we have this ministry, as we received mercy, we do not lose heart, 2 but we have renounced the things hidden because of shame, not walking in craftiness or adulterating the word of God, but by the manifestation of truth commending ourselves to every man's conscience in the sight of God. 3 And even if our gospel is veiled, it is veiled to those who are perishing, 4 in whose case the god of this world has blinded the minds of the unbelieving so that they might not see the light of the gospel of the glory of Christ, who is the image of God. 5 For we do not preach ourselves but Christ Jesus as Lord, and ourselves as your bond-servants for Jesus' sake. 6 For God, who said, "Light shall shine out of darkness," is the One who has shone in our hearts to give the Light of the knowledge of the glory of God in the face of Christ.

7 But we have this treasure in earthen vessels, so that the surpassing greatness of the power will be of God and not from ourselves; 8 *we are* afflicted in every way, but not

crushed; perplexed, but not despairing;[9] persecuted, but not forsaken; struck down, but not destroyed;[10] always carrying about in the body the dying of Jesus, so that the life of Jesus also may be manifested in our body. [11] For we who live are constantly being delivered over to death for Jesus' sake, so that the life of Jesus also may be manifested in our mortal flesh. [12] So death works in us, but life in you.

[13] But having the same spirit of faith, according to what is written, "I BELIEVED, THEREFORE I SPOKE," we also believe, therefore we also speak,[14] knowing that He who raised the Lord Jesus will raise us also with Jesus and will present us with you. [15] For all things *are* for your sakes, so that the grace which is spreading to more and more people may cause the giving of thanks to abound to the glory of God.

[16] Therefore we do not lose heart, but though our outer man is decaying, yet our inner man is being renewed day by day. [17] For momentary, light affliction is producing for us an eternal weight of glory far beyond all comparison, [18] while we look not at the things which are seen, but at the things which are not seen; for the things which are seen are temporal, but the things which are not seen are eternal.

A Personal Ministry (4:1–6)

Paul took personal responsibility for his ministry. He was a commissioned servant who was to communicate the new covenant gospel of grace,[1] whereby the Holy Spirit changed people's hearts and made them righteous before God (2 Cor. 3:6, 8–9). Paul hadn't earned this role but was divinely appointed, even though he'd formerly persecuted the church (Acts 9:1–22), so he felt a keen obligation to fulfill his responsibility. Called by God, Paul had no reason to be discouraged or act cowardly because God supported him with "mercy" (2 Cor. 4:1), a term indicating he perceived his ministry as a gift from God, not a burden to bear. He would not give in to abuse, weariness, reluctance, or timidity; he would not quit.

Though some doubted his integrity and even rejected him, Paul asserted his truthfulness and refusal to distort God's word (4:2). He ministered in contrast to the craftiness (Gr. *panourgia*, "willingness to deceive to accomplish a purpose") of false apostles who invaded the church and demanded payment from parishioners, preaching a health-and-wealth gospel and promoting themselves to gain followers. Paul renounced those ruses. Instead, he vulnerably invited the Corinthians to examine the veracity of his words and the sincerity of his works. He preached for free, edified Christ alone as Lord, and suffered for their sake.

The apostle didn't bring letters of recommendation to the Corinthians (as others did); he brought the evidence of the Spirit's work in his life. For those who doubted him or didn't understand the gospel, Paul wanted to be clear that it wasn't due to his insufficiency, rather, Satan, the "god of this world," hid (i.e., "veiled") the gospel (4:3–4). This clarification primarily referred to Jews who didn't understand Christ as the fulfillment of the Old Testament Messianic prophecies but also applied to any who failed to recognize

Christ as the uniquely perfect and visible representation of the invisible God.

So as not to appear prideful, the apostle reminded the Corinthians of how Christ's lordship was preeminent in Paul's messages (4:5). Even when he encouraged them to imitate him, it was because he was imitating Christ (1 Cor. 11:1). Paul volitionally sacrificed his freedoms and rights (1 Cor. 9:19–23; cf. Mark 8:34–35) as he suffered as their "bond-servant [lit. *slave*] for Jesus' sake" (unlike the false apostles who took advantage of the Corinthians' wealth and generosity).

Paul admitted his sacrificial attitude was not something he could concoct on his own. God, who miraculously spoke light into darkness (Genesis 1:3), had shone in his heart with the "Light of the knowledge of the glory of God in the face of Christ" (2 Cor. 4:6), a triple reference to Isaiah 9:2, Jesus' claim as the "Light of the World" (John 8:12), and his own Damascus Road experience (Acts 9:1–19). By "shining" in Paul's heart the understanding of Jesus as Lord, God had removed the blindness caused by Satan, exposed Paul's sinful condition (cf. Ephesians 5:13–14), thus purifying and making him new. Paul sincerely wanted the same for the Corinthians (see sidebar "Literary Contrasts").

A Valuable Treasure (4:7–12)

Paul's first-century audience used pottery lamps into which were fitted wicks and oil for burning. Perhaps as they read the words, "God . . . shone in our hearts," the Corinthians imagined light emanating from their clay lamps. If so, it was a beautiful use of imagery. Although Paul had the light of Christ, he knew he had not yet achieved Christlikeness (Philippians 3:12; 2 Cor. 3:18). He was a fallible, ordinary, meager repository for God's amazing, redemptive work.

Herein lies the first of several paradoxes of the Christian journey Paul's words depict. God placed the "treasure" of his saving work in humanity, "earthen vessels" (4:7a). The gospel's indescribable value is in people who make mistakes and dishonor God! Paul wasn't espousing the Gnostic idea that all physical matter is inherently evil; he was acknowledging the distinction of God's glory versus his own weakness and propensity toward sin (Romans 3:23). God has a purpose behind this contrast: the demonstration of his power, which far surpasses humanity's strength or ability (2 Cor. 4:7b; 12:9).

To prove his vulnerability, Paul listed several paradoxes in 2 Corinthians 4:8–9. He mentions experiences and human weaknesses that don't naturally match the emotions or reality connected to them because God's absolute power is working. Each of those, in the Corinthians' minds, would likely summon images of gladiators or military battle—appropriate, since believers wage war against Satan (Eph. 6:10ff). Paul was:

- "afflicted in every way [i.e., compressed], but not crushed;
- perplexed [i.e., at a loss], but not despairing[2];
- persecuted [i.e., hunted], but not forsaken[3];

- struck down, but not destroyed."

Paul continued with another paradox in 2 Corinthians 4:10–11,[4] explaining that he (and those with him) were always near death (cf. 2 Cor. 1:8–10; 1 Cor. 4:9; 15:30–31) but never lifeless. Paul not only preached Christ's sacrifice; he lived sacrificially. However, death did not conquer Christ, nor would it defeat Paul. Paul concluded, "death works in us, but life in you" (2 Cor. 4:12). As he suffered, enduring multiple near-death experiences, the Corinthians enjoyed increased hope and conviction by seeing God faithfully undergird Paul (cf. 2 Cor. 1:6).

A Fearless Hope in a Confident Future (4:13–18)

By way of celebrating God's trustworthiness, and because he shared the same faith as the ancient psalmist, the Apostle Paul fell back on his Jewish roots and paraphrased Psalm 116:10's declaration: "I believed, therefore I spoke," explaining why he must continue to testify of God's deliverance (2 Cor. 4:13). He persevered because he was confident that God, who raised Jesus from the dead, would, in the final resurrection, raise all believers (4:14). Paul persevered because he believed in his ministry's eternal impact. Everything he did and experienced was for the sake of others. His desire was that they would glorify God by giving thanks for his grace, resulting in the gospel spreading to more and more people (4:15). Love for people motivated Paul, just as Christ's love motivated him to endure the cross so we might be reconciled to God (Colossians 1:20). Multitudes may have never heard the gospel if Paul had run away from the danger and risks he encountered.

Grace received prompts thanksgiving, and thanksgiving engenders humility. As these increased, Paul saw reason for hope. He refused to grow discouraged or neglect his ministerial responsibilities (cf. Galatians 6:9; 2 Thessalonians 3:13; Hebrews 12:3), even though ministry had taken a physical toll on his body (the temporal, fleshly "outer man"). In fact, Paul's soul (the eternal, spiritual "inner man") found rejuvenation as he saw God glorified and his own Christlikeness increased through his difficulties (2 Cor. 4:16). This rejuvenation is yet another paradox of the Christian faith journey. However, it's a gradual process. The phrase "day by day" means slow, repetitive development or transformation (often regrouping and trying again), not merely accomplishing a progressive step-by-step program.

This growth in fellowship with Christ and the Holy's Spirit's power, prompted resilience, and enabled Paul to perceive his trials with a different perspective than most of us, which is another faith paradox. Paul called them "momentary, light affliction[s]" (4:17). The apostle didn't trivialize or feign indifference to the seriousness of his struggles,[5] nor did he imply all Christians must suffer as he did. Instead, he put his tribulations in their proper place: inconsequential when compared to eternal glory (Rom. 8:18). The afflictions were actually "producing" (Gr. *katergazetai*, *affecting, bringing out as a result*) an "eternal weight of glory far beyond all comparison" (see sidebar "An Eternal Weight of Glory"). It is almost as though Paul pulled out an imaginary scale and weighed his afflictions (cf. 2 Cor. 1:8) versus his future delight, and the scale readily revealed his coming glory as far superior to the gravity of his struggles.

The Corinthians, however, mistakenly thought Paul's struggles disproved that he was growing in Christlikeness. However, rather than berating them, the apostle gently instructed them as a spiritual father, explaining this Christian mystery. The Corinthians were looking at what they could see (4:18), the "temporal" (i.e., Paul's physical appearance, the emotional toll and mental strain from his struggles), rather than what they could not see, the "eternal" (i.e., the peace and security generated in his relationship with Christ and his future reward in heaven).[6] For Paul, the result of his suffering rested confidently in God's mighty hand, who was working all things for good (Rom. 8:28). This perspective of the future glory Paul anticipated gave him joyful security in God's calling and the Spirit's work in and through him, regardless of the lack of success, circumstances, or people who challenged him in his ministry. His focus was on his future with Christ. Ours should be too.

Implications and Actions

Many of us lack an intimate knowledge of God and his word, not fully grasping the splendor of life with God for eternity. Thus, our perspective is shortsighted, and in ignorance we focus on gaining (or at least not losing) as much as possible during our lives. When we do, we limit our service, refuse to love sacrificially, prioritize temporal non-essentials, and seek to store up treasures on earth (Matt. 6:19), labeling them as blessings.

Assured of God's faithfulness, Paul looked forward to hearing God say, "Well done" (Matt. 25:21). He didn't "lose heart" because the eternal glory he anticipated outweighed the burdens he faced and the prospect of prosperity here. Eternal glory was not only a place in heaven with the God he worshiped, but with the people to whom he had ministered and for whom he had suffered.

Fundamentally, ministry isn't about schedules, dollars, or programs but people. Unfortunately, until we're in heaven, people will frustrate and disappoint us. Our passionate area of service may not excite others. Those we serve may not appreciate the hours of sacrifice we've poured into meeting their needs. How we react to these people and the challenges they bring is greatly influenced by our eternal ministry perspective. Focus on the long-term goal and don't lose heart.

Literary Contrasts

Even with in-depth study, it's easy to miss Paul's beautiful literary contrast between 2 Corinthians 4:4 (what Satan does) and 2 Corinthians 4:6 (what God does). We've placed them side-by-side for a straightforward visual:

... the god of this world	For God
has blinded	who said, "Light shall shine
the minds of the unbelieving	out of darkness,"
so that they might not see	is the One who has shone
the light of the gospel	in our hearts
of the glory of Christ	to give
who is the image of God.	the Light of the knowledge
	of the glory of God
	in the face of Christ.

An Eternal Weight of Glory

In 1941, author and biblical apologist C. S. Lewis preached a sermon entitled, "The Weight of Glory." Lewis suggested glory meant either fame or luminosity. "[S]ince to be famous means to be better known than other people," he said, "the desire for fame appears to me of hell rather than heaven. As for the second, who wishes to become a kind of living electric light bulb?" Eventually, Lewis determined glory to be "fame with God, approval or appreciation by God."[7]

Lewis posited that God created humanity to long for his delight and approval (Matt. 25:21), for heaven, and the rewards accompanying a life well-lived. Unfortunately, many of us live as though life on Earth is the end-goal and her prizes our greatest reward.

Although written in Greek, Paul's "eternal weight of glory" had double meaning, since in Hebrew *glory* also meant "weighty" or "heaviness." Thus, Paul contrasted ministry's present pressures as brief and slight, while doubly stressing the long-lasting significance of God's delight. Apparently, the relationship between the two is proportional. The greater the afflictions, the grander the glory.

Questions

1. What is your personal ministry? What do you feel a calling or conviction toward? Are you executing your responsibility? What excuses are you offering for not ministering?

2. Examine Paul's detailed list of sufferings (2 Cor. 11:21–33) and compare it to your own. Does it help to reset or change your mind about your struggles? Do you feel as though you can say with Paul that your vulnerabilities (2 Cor. 4:8–11) are compensated by God's strength? Why or why not?

3. What challenges are you currently facing in your ministry role? How does Paul's example help you? How can you reshape your perspective to be more eternal? Who is watching you to see God's power revealed through your weaknesses?

4. Identify modern spiritual leaders who teach a "health-and-wealth gospel." Use quotes from them to support your conclusion.

5. Although we as ministers (whether laypersons or vocationally employed) may be connected to a body of believers, we answer to Christ, not the church. How do we know we are pleasing him?

6. Are you judging one of Christ's servants harshly or placing unfair expectations on him or her?

7. How often do you think about heaven and the future we'll have there? Is it something you look forward to with longing or eagerness, or fear because of uncertainty? Do you find you're sufficiently happy here on earth and not particularly drawn toward eternity?

8. What challenges have you faced in your ministry for the Lord?

9. Why is it hard to have an eternal focus?

10. How has God provided you with confidence during ministry challenges?

11. Who is struggling in their ministry who could use your encouragement?

NOTES

1. As opposed to the old covenant of law which Christ fulfilled (cf. Matt. 5:17).

2. This is the same word used in 2 Corinthians 1:8, where Paul *did* despair of losing his life. Clearly what happened in Asia grew him to the point of no longer despairing. Even Paul had areas for spiritual growth!

3. This is from the same translated word Jesus cried out on the cross in Matthew 27:46.

4. Notice the preeminence of Jesus' name in these two verses. Clearly, Paul looks to Jesus' human example of endurance (as opposed to his divine nature of omnipotence) as he endures difficulty. Jesus came as a suffering servant (Is. 52:13—53:12), and Paul expects no less as his apostle. Likewise, the same power that raised Jesus from the dead lives in him (Rom. 8:11).

5. Believers are free to avoid suffering and persecution when it won't hinder or compromise our faith or testimony. Furthermore, Scripture certainly encourages us to pray for healing when sick and deliverance when needed (cf. John 10:31,39; Acts 9:25; Phil. 4:4–7; James 5:14).

6. Jewish thought concluded adversity was the result of sin or condemnation by God. Likewise, Corinthian culture taught suffering revealed the presence of evil or punishment for disobedience, and comfort or well-being indicated blessing by the gods. Unfortunately, the modern reality is that most Westernized, evangelical believers and church-attenders believe the same principle is at work in Christianity. In fact, several well-known modern preachers advocate this idea that God's greatest desire for us is our physical well-being and financial prosperity, known as the "Health and Wealth Gospel."

7. https://www.verber.com/mark/xian/weight-of-glory.pdf. (Accessed 1/7/2018).

lesson 11

Giving and Receiving Criticism

MAIN IDEA

Being able to properly give and receive criticism is a part of Christian maturity.

QUESTION TO EXPLORE

How can I give and receive criticism in a proper manner?

STUDY AIM

To comprehend how to give and receive criticism in a proper manner

QUICK READ

Many Christians are either too blunt or refuse to criticize at all for fear of offending or creating drama. Paul demonstrated how to share and receive criticism appropriately.

Introduction

This lesson's Scripture passage, 2 Corinthians 7:5–16, is one side of a conversation about giving and receiving criticism. Paul's initial criticism and the Corinthians' reaction are obviously discernable, and Paul's secondary response is explicit.

Paul wrote multiple letters to the Corinthians. Most scholars believe he wrote between four and six. At least one, known as the "severe letter" or the "harsh letter," is missing (referenced in 2 Corinthians 2:4 and 7:8). The Corinthian church had many problems, which led to more letters from Paul than he wrote to any other church. Even though the Corinthians had a host of issues, including some animosity toward Paul, Paul's love is evident in his unwillingness to give up on this church. Paul provided an example of how to deal with conflict, whether that conflict is in the church, family, marriage, friendship, or workplace.[1]

2 Corinthians 7:5–16

5 For when we came into Macedonia, this body of ours had no rest, but we were harassed at every turn—conflicts on the outside, fears within. 6 But God, who comforts the downcast, comforted us by the coming of Titus, 7 and not only by his coming but also by the comfort you had given him. He told us about your longing for me, your deep sorrow, your ardent concern for me, so that my joy was greater than ever.

[8] Even if I caused you sorrow by my letter, I do not regret it. Though I did regret it—I see that my letter hurt you, but only for a little while—[9] yet now I am happy, not because you were made sorry, but because your sorrow led you to repentance. For you became sorrowful as God intended and so were not harmed in any way by us. [10] Godly sorrow brings repentance that leads to salvation and leaves no regret, but worldly sorrow brings death. [11] See what this godly sorrow has produced in you: what earnestness, what eagerness to clear yourselves, what indignation, what alarm, what longing, what concern, what readiness to see justice done. At every point you have proved yourselves to be innocent in this matter. [12] So even though I wrote to you, it was not on account of the one who did the wrong or of the injured party, but rather that before God you could see for yourselves how devoted to us you are. [13] By all this we are encouraged. [14] In addition to our own encouragement, we were especially delighted to see how happy Titus was, because his spirit has been refreshed by all of you. I had boasted to him about you, and you have not embarrassed me. But just as everything we said to you was true, so our boasting about you to Titus has proved to be true as well. [15] And his affection for you is all the greater when he remembers that you were all obedient, receiving him with fear and trembling. [16] I am glad I can have complete confidence in you.

Realize Everyone Lives in a Certain Context (7:5–7)

Everyone lives in a certain context (situation), including you. In these two verses Paul wrote of the Corinthians' problems, as well as his own: no rest, harassed, conflicts, fears, down-cast, longing, deep sorrow, and concern.

Paul had a context in which he was living and writing from, and he knew the Corinthians had a backdrop of their own. Each person's context includes difficulties or challenges related to health, finances, stress, relationships, sin, and other things. Paul knew of his situation and, in his graciousness, he understood the readers of his letter were experiencing their own challenges. The ESV translates the last part of verse 5 as, "fightings without and fears within,"[2] which describes the personal conflict all people face at one time or another. Understanding this context allows individuals to see one another as fallible humans in need of love and sympathy.

Lesson one of "giving and receiving criticism" is to understand the context of everyone involved. It reminds everyone to clearly assess themselves first and then imagine "walking in the shoes of another" before jumping to conclusions or critiques.

Do Not Ignore Conflict (7:8–9)

There are times to overlook issues, and then there are times when each Christian must engage for the sake of peace. Pray for discernment for when to do both. Everyone appreciates a peacemaker over someone who creates dissention, but being a peacemaker is not the same thing as being a "peace-faker." The latter fakes harmony out of fear or laziness for a while, as long as it is convenient or until unresolved issues fester long enough to do severe damage. A peacemaker knows when to overlook the insignificant, but also when it is necessary to deal with conflict.

Paul wrote his exacting letter in agony, knowing it would cause distress for the church at Corinth, but he could not ignore their issues. By not ignoring their state of affairs, Paul was proactive and dealt with the troubles head-on. Many issues that lead to conflict germinate from inaction and passivity, allowing unnamed or hidden agendas to grow into unmanageable situations. Conflict is the natural result of any two groups or people coming together. Graciously giving criticism allows both parties to deal with the issues at hand.

Caution is warranted. The standard responses to conflict are fight or flight. Some people will fight over every issue in a relationship, in a family, at work, or even in church. Others will walk away without telling anyone why. The latter chooses flight instead of any level of conflict. Neither approach is biblical. God calls us into community with one another and to treat one another with love, kindness, and gentleness. We are not to abandon one another. The more disciplined approach instead of fight or flight is to honestly, but in a godly manner, deal with issues as they arise. In Ephesians 4:15, Paul wrote we should be "speaking the truth in love." The same principle applies when we encounter conflict.

Allow for Godly Sorrow (7:10–11)

It is a good thing to live in an era that emphasizes respect, care, and the avoidance of offending others. Few want to say or do anything that might hurt someone. Though this is admirable, the extreme is that Christians are afraid to confront one another. Even when confrontation is necessary and taken, there is the tendency to attempt to quickly heal the wound. Paul, on the other hand, knew that it was good for the Corinthians to experience authentic sorrow so that God could bring them to repentance.

There is a different between godly sorrow and worldly regret or mortification. Worldly regret and mortification for being "found out" are self-centered reactions that lead to guilt and shame, usually generated from getting caught in a compromising situation. It often develops into paralyzed fear, destruction, isolation, and inaction within the person and sometimes beyond them.

Godly sorrow leads to contrition, repentance, and ultimately to change. This sorrow is true remorse for the original action. Godly sorrow is allowing oneself to be in the presence of the Holy Spirit's conviction, counseling, and eventual comforting. It develops into action and change—such as strength, confidence, sympathy, community, and mutual spiritual growth.

Godly sorrow leads to life and transformation that is beneficial for the individual, his or her community, and the kingdom of God. Worldly regret is demoralizing self-pity benefitting no one and ultimately leading to death (7:10). Worldly regret leads to unresolved guilt like that of Judas, mortification that caused him to run away from God and to ultimately take his life. Godly sorrow leads to conviction like that of Peter, who ran to God after his denial of Jesus and ultimately fulfilled his life mission.

Look for Solutions (7:11–12)

Paul wrote, "See what this sorrow has produced in you" (7:11), indicating that his criticism had the value of producing something positive. Giving and receiving criticism should have the end goal of finding solutions to problems or faults, not just griping for the sake of griping. It is not looking for blame, nor it is personal. Paul did not mention the names of those involved in this incident (7:12), unlike when he named Demas for desertion and Alexander the metalworker for harming him in 2 Timothy 4:10, 14; or even when he confronted the Apostle Peter in Galatians 2:11. By not naming those involved in this incident, Paul was protecting them because they had resolved the issue. The apostle's criticism led them to repentance and a solution.

Likewise, the goal of criticism today should not be to embarrass others or set them up for personal blame, but rather to find common ground and productive solutions to the problems that plague our marriages, families, churches, communities, and country. Name-calling and personal attacks may be popular in social media, on television, or perhaps even in person, but they do not produce effective solutions. To build the kingdom of God, we need to seek spiritual solutions.

Another vital aspect of seeking solutions is to discard no one. To not get personal or blame others, Paul refused to write-off anyone in the Corinthian story. We get frustrated, and at times, we can conclude someone is beyond redemption or restoration. Often in these cases, our criticism is not motivated by seeking a solution as much as it looks to assign blame and to dismiss the other person. It is helpful to consider that every person lives in a discreet context, even those whom we want to dismiss—dealing with their own problems, consequences, or perhaps even the sin or darkness that envelops them. Comparing the context of others to our lives may help foster sympathy, compassion, and good solutions for everyone.

Response Is Necessary (7:13)

Paul could not control how the Corinthians would respond. He waited fretfully for their response. Titus' report that they responded well to Paul's criticism, repented, and changed their ways brought joy to all involved, especially Paul.

The Corinthians could have been furious with Paul and rebuffed his criticism or fired shots back at him, which would have delayed or maybe even ended any attempt at a viable solution. Sometimes, even if our criticism is respectful and beneficial, it may not be received well. We must be aware of that and be prepared for a positive or negative result. If the issue is of great consequence, then we should voice our concerns. Our fidelity in the matter should not be weighed based on a possible negative response. Hopefully, it will lead to a joyous occasion like Paul, Titus, and the Corinthians experienced. It is good to know that, ultimately, not everything is in our control.

Resolution Is Possible (7:14–16)

The relationship between Paul and the Corinthians was contentious at times. There was a reason Paul waited anxiously for the response Titus brought back. The Corinthians could have rejected Paul and his legitimate criticism. That possible rejection did not keep Paul from dealing with the Corinthian issues. Nevertheless, he waited for an outcome that could go one of two ways. The verdict was resolution. The issue was solved as they had received Titus (and Paul's instruction) with fear and trembling (verse 15). Resolution is always possible if we are faithful to handle problems the right way. Do not give up on a problematic relationship. Resolution is possible.

The highest form of resolution is a full restoration in which the relationship rift is fully healed. This is always the goal, but not always the result. It appears Paul and the Corinthians experienced restoration. Resolution may involve a change in the culture that created the conflict but not necessarily restoration of the relationship. We cannot have restoration if we stay in a relational "fight-or-flight" mode. We must be sensitive as well as bold enough to appropriately give and receive criticism, dealing with the issues that we must while learning to overlook the insignificant.

Implications and Actions

There are issues that affect the overall health of relationships: marriage, families, community, school, work, and church. We can overlook, ignore, inflame, or handle them in a godly fashion. The issues may involve theological debates, working practices, personal differences, or offenses. Paul's interaction with the Corinthians provides a high-quality example of how to humbly and lovingly confront issues with the goal of resolving conflict without hurting the relationship—or perhaps restoring it if necessary. Speaking the truth in love reveals honest caring when those with whom we share our lives are confronted with kindness and respect.

The Joyous Effect of Godly Sorrow

Famous British Baptist Preacher F. B. Meyer (1847–1929) wrote "The Joyous Effect of Godly Sorrow" based on 2 Corinthians 7:5–16. In it, he talked about Paul's anxiety of sending this criticism: "Paul's tender heart had been rent with anxiety lest the Corinthian church should resent its terms and be alienated from his friendship." But Meyer knew what Paul knew, "He felt also that their sorrow was of the true and genuine sort, which does not consist of mere mortification at being found out or of the dread of punishment, but which implies a profound hatred of sin as grieving the Holy Savior and unworthy of his precious blood." Godly sorrow comes from our offense of God's Spirit and goodness within us. Therefore, repentance is the restoration of who we are supposed to be in Christ. According to Meyer, the purpose of this sorrow is that the believer, "puts away the wrong, and with chastened steps comes again into the way of the sacred Cross."[3]

Levels of Resolution

1. Simple Forgiveness: forgiveness but nothing more; relationship may not be restored
2. Protective Forgiveness: forgiveness, but boundaries must be established to prevent future issues
3. Working Restoration: forgiveness, but restoration is a process that will take time
4. Partial Restoration: forgiveness and reestablished hopeful, but guarded relationship
5. Full Restoration: forgiveness and restored relationship of love and trust

Note that at every level, the offense or conflict may never be forgotten, but it can still be overcome.

Questions

1. What part of your current context may be leaving you vulnerable, and cause issues that may affect others? Consider a person at work, in your family, or even at church with whom you have an issue. Now, consider his or her context. What about their context might be contributing to their issues?

2. Discuss what discernment is needed to know the difference between overlooking an offense or problem, compared to when you cannot ignore it and must confront a situation.

3. Have you experienced godly sorrow? Describe what sorrow looks like to you.

4. What is the difference between destructive criticism and productive criticism that leads to solutions?

5. Have you experienced the various levels of conflict resolution and restoration? Describe what happened.

NOTES

1. Unless otherwise indicated, all Scripture quotations in lessons 11–13 are from the New International Version (1984 edition).

2. Scripture quotation is from The ESV® Bible (The Holy Bible, English Standard Version®), copyright © 2001 by Crossway, a publishing ministry of Good News Publishers. Used by permission. All rights reserved.

3. http://biblehub.com/commentaries/ttb/2_corinthians/7.htm. (Accessed 5/27/18).

lesson  12

Dealing with Disputes

MAIN IDEA

Solving disputes in the church requires integrity in motives and methods.

QUESTION TO EXPLORE

How can we solve disputes in the church?

STUDY AIM

To affirm integrity in motives and methods as a prerequisite for solving church disputes

QUICK READ

Disputes are inevitable. Paul had an ongoing set of issues with the Corinthians. In solving them, he demonstrated when to be diplomatic and how to share the truth in love.

Introduction

I once sat in a church business meeting that erupted into an argument over the cost of a vacuum cleaner. The volunteer cleaning the church paid $162.00 for a vacuum cleaner and reported the purchase on the monthly financial statement. Another member knew that the same vacuum cleaner had been on sale at another store for $148.00 and protested the church irresponsibly paid the additional $14.00. Harsh things were said. Feelings were bruised. The rest of the meeting had a cloud of melancholy hanging over it that lasted through the following Bible study. It was a complete waste of time for everyone who came that evening. I wanted to pull a twenty-dollar bill out of my pocket and cover the overage, but I worried that would only increase the tension.

Sadly, such silly disputes happen in many families and churches. There are also disagreements about more significant matters that affect the cause of Christ. Paul dealt with such a dispute in 2 Corinthians 10.

2 Corinthians 10

1 By the meekness and gentleness of Christ, I appeal to you—I, Paul, who am "timid" when face to face with you, but "bold" when away! **2** I beg you that when I come I may not have to be as bold as I expect to be toward some people who think that we live by the standards of this world. **3** For though we live in the world, we do not wage war as the world does.

4 The weapons we fight with are not the weapons of the world. On the contrary, they have divine power to demolish strongholds. **5** We demolish arguments and every pretension that sets itself up against the knowledge of God, and we take captive every thought to make it obedient to Christ. **6** And we will be ready to punish every act of disobedience, once your obedience is complete.

7 You are looking only on the surface of things. If anyone is confident that he belongs to Christ, he should consider again that we belong to Christ just as much as he. **8** For even if I boast somewhat freely about the authority the Lord gave us for building you up rather than pulling you down, I will not be ashamed of it. **9** I do not want to seem to be trying to frighten you with my letters. **10** For some say, "His letters are weighty and forceful, but in person he is unimpressive and his speaking amounts to nothing." **11** Such people should realize that what we are in our letters when we are absent, we will be in our actions when we are present.

12 We do not dare to classify or compare ourselves with some who commend themselves. When they measure themselves by themselves and compare themselves with themselves, they are not wise. **13** We, however, will not boast beyond proper limits, but will confine our boasting to the field God has assigned to us, a field that reaches even to you. **14** We are not going too far in our boasting, as would be the case if we had not come to you, for we did get as far as you with the gospel of Christ. **15** Neither do we go beyond our limits by boasting of work done by others. Our hope is that, as your faith continues to grow, our area of activity among you will greatly expand, **16** so that we can preach the gospel in the regions beyond you. For we do not want to boast about work already done in another man's territory. [17] But, "Let him who boasts boast in the Lord." [18] For it is not the one who commends himself who is approved, but the one whom the Lord commends.

Use Diplomacy to Deal with Disputes (10:1–2)

Paul had been gentle with the Corinthians when he was with them in person out of kindness and diplomacy. That soft approach backfired when he had to write to them more bluntly. His accusers used the differences in his tone (when he was with and away from the Corinthians), to attack him and discredit his genuineness. The difference in his demeanor demonstrated that an astute person, and especially a good leader, needs to know when to be gentle and when to be direct.

Paul's earlier humility was not a sign of weakness but a show of restraint. He was allowing for a growth process to take place within the Corinthians. Upon hearing that the growth had not occurred, but instead that they regressed in matters of discipleship, Paul then took a more plain-spoken and firm tone. In the brevity of the letter, he did not beat around the bush, but dealt with issues head-on and with some force. It was the same Paul, but the circumstance warranted a different response.

We must be diplomatic in our relationships because we represent Christ. In fact, we may be the only representative of Jesus with whom some people interact. To be diplomatic, we must be slow to anger, gentle in temperament, patient with others' faults, humble in our shortcomings, and tolerant of mistakes as we guide others. We must do so as leaders in the church, in the home, and in the community. There are certain times to have a righteous indignation and assertive response, but those times should be rare for two reasons:

1. We lessen the impact of when we do have to be direct if we are candid about everything.

2. We lose the ear of those around us if we consistently use a harsh and demanding tone.

Paul reminded the Corinthians that believers do not live by the standards of this world (10:2), but that faith causes us to deal with others in a godly way. This world fights and claws for recognition, control, and power. Jesus said the first must be last and that the leader must serve others (Matthew 20:25–27). Paul affirmed that this spiritual pattern is normative within the church, instead of the worldly standard of power.

Unfortunately, too many laypersons and church leaders are more like Paul's accusers in Corinth. They are caught up in the political power struggle that has limited lasting value and misses the eternal standards Jesus established. Paul was diplomatic for the sake of all involved, but he had to handle the situation as his authority demanded.

Be Aware of Spiritual Warfare in Disputes (10:3–6)

As believers, we do not wage war as this world does, and we do not use the weapons of the world. The world uses anger, rage, wrath, threat, manipulation, coercion, jealousy, power, money, lies, and sex as weapons. The followers of Christ have been called to use love, kindness, service, sacrifice, humility, peace, faith, and truth as our weapons.

Paul cataloged what we need in Ephesians 6:13–18—the full armor of God: the belt of truth, the breastplate of righteousness, sandals of the gospel of peace, the shield of faith, the helmet of salvation and the sword of the Spirit. Paul was going up against more than just his human adversaries. Paul recognized spiritual opposition to our work. It can be blatant and overt, but it can also be subtle and subversive. It can have a human or organizational face, or it can be an invisible empire working against us and the kingdom of God. Nevertheless, one should never give up hope because divine power will demolish every stronghold (10:4).

There is a balance between living in fear of the "devil-behind-every-rock" theology versus the complete denial of any satanic reality. Paul was cautiously and prudently aware of Satan's schemes (Eph. 6:11), but he wholly trusted in the power of God to lead us to victory.

2 Corinthians 10:4 provides the hope that God will destroy our strongholds if we surrender them to him. What strongholds have a strangling grip on you? Addictions such as drugs, alcohol, pornography, gambling, eating disorders,

greed, materialism, insatiable appetites for sex, power, money, and fame are strongholds in many of our lives. Strongholds grip churches, communities, and cultures which seem like insurmountable challenges. These strongholds lead directly to disputes and conflicts in our relationships.

Some people have given up ever conquering strongholds or have given up rescuing loved ones from their control. Paul commanded us not to give up. God has the power to demolish every stronghold. The word "demolish" is translated from the Greek *kathaireo*, which means "to pull down or take down entirely without leaving anything standing." Such is the outcome of our strongholds if we allow God to have constant control of our lives. We must continually take up our armor and be active partners with God. Without it, we will be unable to extinguish Satan's fiery darts (Eph. 6:16).

2 Corinthians 10:5 gives us the command we need to allow God to take down the strongholds. We must "take captive every thought." The more we let our thoughts linger on negative things, the more we relinquish the power of God to take down those strongholds. Paul's imagery of every thought is a good one. He indicates that the process of victory is won through the focus of our attention, capturing negative thoughts and vanquishing them at the cross. Spiritual success is not achieved with a grandiose gesture but in a countless series of surrenders.

Punishment awaits those who are disobedient and refuse to yield control over to God. This judgment is inevitable for the individual in his or her struggles as well, as in the more substantial disputes within a family, community, and the church.

The church must not allow underlying spiritual warfare to erode its communal bond and kingdom purpose. Church leaders must work together and through prayer, diplomacy, love, and cooperation submit to God's authority to win the day against spiritual warfare.

Be Straightforward in Disputes (10:7–11)

Paul urged the Corinthian believers to consider the matter more deeply than just what others were whispering in their ears. How often are churches, workplaces, and families torn apart by the whisper campaigns going on behind the backs of others? Paul wrote his forceful letter to take control of the situation and declare his authority in Christ. What he said would be backed up when he would next come to them in person. He was not ashamed of his vigor because he used it as he has needed to convey the truth. Paul's straightforwardness and severe tone were necessary because the Corinthians continued to defiantly ignore the godly expectations the apostle consistently set before them.

We must not give wishy-washy answers to others that create ambiguous expectations. We do not have to be rude or overbearing for the sake of hurting others, but we must make certain the point of living Christlike lives. Paul's use of diplomacy, mixed with forthright communication, is a model for all of us.

Resolve Disputes to Get On with the Greater Purpose (10:12–18)

Paul wanted to resolve the lingering issues within the Corinthian church for the benefit of the church body, but also so that they could be the platform for spreading the gospel. His boasting was not for the sake of self-promotion but for the sake of the Corinthians. He wanted them to understand his authority, position, and hopes for them. His boasting was in the field God had assigned to him.

He was the apostle to the Gentiles (Eph. 3:1 and 1 Timothy 2:7). The Corinthian church was partly a fruit of that calling. Paul was looking for how his ministry would continue to expand within the Corinthian community. Even beyond that, Paul was excited by how the gospel would be preached in regions beyond them. That goal would not be possible if his work or their faithfulness fell flat. The higher purpose was not who was right or who got credit, but the singularity of the gospel message's influence to spread and develop in existing and new areas.

Likewise, we must look beyond our disputes to get on with the higher purpose God has for us, our local ministries, and the broader kingdom purposes. Often our conflicts are nothing more than preferences and petty arguments that distract us from becoming what we need to be in service to the Lord. Satan can claim victory once our effectiveness wanes. We do not have to be eliminated if our usefulness is gone.

Implications and Actions

Whether the dispute is over the cost of a vacuum cleaner or something more serious, there are principles for how to handle conflicts that will arise in our relationships. We must seek to be diplomatic without relinquishing truth. We must be straightforward in our conversations, not indecisive while working to a resolution. The resolution must serve the higher purpose of God's plan for us and our families and ministries. We must seek this resolution knowing there will always be an adversary attempting to disrupt God's work through us; therefore, we must still be on our guard against spiritual warfare.

Charles Haddon Spurgeon

In his sermon, "Forts Demolished, and Prisoners Taken," British Baptist Preacher C. H. Spurgeon (1834–1892) listed five garrisoned fortresses that need to be torn down for the human heart to be penetrated by the true knowledge of God.

1. Those who do not want to know God.
2. Those who think that they already know Him.
3. Those who think they do not need any help finding God.
4. Those who think they know something better than God.
5. Those who are in despair and think that they can never know God.

These strongholds can be torn down by the gospel. As Spurgeon said, "This is the great object for which the gospel is sent into the world—that the knowledge of the glory of God may cover the earth as the waters cover the sea." He also listed a series of thoughts to be led away into captivity: hopes, fears, memory, powers of meditation, desires and aspirations, plots and designs, love and hate, and fancy (imagination).[1]

Dealing with Disputes

Imagine someone at work has unfairly criticized you in a meeting regarding a tough decision you had to make, but you are sure the individual does not know the privileged details that you cannot share. How would you diplomatically, but candidly, resolve this situation in a Christlike manner, either in private or in public?

Questions

1. Who has the gift of diplomacy, able to lead without offending or selling short the issue at hand? How can we be more like that person?

2. Describe the balance between keeping an awareness of spiritual warfare without living in constant fear.

3. How can we fail to settle disputes because of a lack of forthright conversations? What is the result of giving mixed, unclear signals and directions?

4. Give an example of how unresolved disputes can disrupt the higher purposes God has set.

5. Share experiences of how you have resolved a situation that led to more impactful ministry.

NOTES

1. "Forts Demolished, and Prisoners Taken," British Baptist Preacher C. H. Spurgeon [Sermon no. 1473, May 11, 1879.]

lesson 13

The Promise of Sufficient Grace

MAIN IDEA

God's powerful grace is sufficient to meet our needs.

QUESTION TO EXPLORE

How does the power of God's grace prove sufficient to meet our needs?

STUDY AIM

To trust the power of God's grace to be sufficient to meet my needs

QUICK READ

Life has tough times. God's provision will take care of us through those days. His powerful grace is sufficient to meet all our needs.

Introduction

Life is full of uncertain, stressful days and seasons. God knows our difficulties, and he cares about us, especially in our most desperate times. He has given us his sufficient grace to carry us through challenging days. His grace is more than enough to strengthen us to to handle all that we will endure. We must not rest on our strength but experience the all-sustaining presence of God.

2 Corinthians 12:1–10

¹ I must go on boasting. Although there is nothing to be gained, I will go on to visions and revelations from the Lord. ² I know a man in Christ who fourteen years ago was caught up to the third heaven. Whether it was in the body or out of the body I do not know—God knows. ³ And I know that this man—whether in the body or apart from the body I do not know, but God knows— ⁴ was caught up to paradise. He heard inexpressible things, things that man is not permitted to tell. ⁵ I will boast about a man like that, but I will not boast about myself, except about my weaknesses. ⁶ Even if I should choose to boast, I would not be a fool, because I would be speaking the truth. But I refrain, so no one will think more of me than is warranted by what I do or say.

⁷ To keep me from becoming conceited because of these surpassingly great revelations, there was given me a thorn in my flesh, a messenger of Satan, to torment me. ⁸ Three times I pleaded with the Lord to take it away from me. ⁹ But he said

to me, "My grace is sufficient for you, for my power is made perfect in weakness." Therefore I will boast all the more gladly about my weaknesses, so that Christ's power may rest on me. **10** That is why, for Christ's sake, I delight in weaknesses, in insults, in hardships, in persecutions, in difficulties. For when I am weak, then I am strong.

Paul Wrote of His Experience with God (12:1–6)

Paul was talking about himself when he, wrote, "I know a man," but he used the third person to humbly deflect attention while speaking of the honor of having had such an experience with God. His critics could not match his experience, nevertheless, the story was about the work of God, not the apostle. Paul had at least four amazing experiences with God beyond the one he referenced here (Acts 9:3–7; 16:9; 18:9–10; 22:17–21), and these five validated his credentials as a spiritual authority; however, Paul stressed that he could not, and would not, boast.

There was no boasting in spiritual pedigree or in personal accomplishments, only in what God had done. The boasting for the latter was not for selfish embellishment but to lift up the work and magnificence of God. Paul's sole boast was that he was a vessel used for God's purpose. If there were any boasting, it was that God brought him into his presence. Even then, Paul highlighted his human weakness.

For us to experience the sufficient grace of God, we must first encounter God. It would be fantastic to undergo a heavenly encounter as Paul did, but those incidents occurred at the time the new church was transitioning from a small, exclusive sect within Judaism into a worldwide movement. Yes, God can still speak through visions and dreams, but these are not necessary for us to have our experiences with God today. We have the advantage of the New Testament and a fully-formed church body added to the Holy Spirit. The Holy Spirit was Paul's sole guide through those encounters. Our firsthand experiences and revelation can be just as real and vital as Paul's were, laying for us a foundation of grace that leads to peace and sufficiency.

Paul's experience in heaven speaks of his encounter with God. The apostle said he was caught up into heaven and paradise. Throughout his writings, Paul had a lot to say about heaven. It is where the angels live (Galatians 1:8). It is where Jesus came from (Ephesians 4:9; Romans 10:6) and to where he returned (Eph. 4:10; 6:9; Colossians 4:1, Rom. 8:34) and from where he will come to Earth again (Philippians 3:20; 1 Thessalonians 1:10; 4:16; 2 Thess. 1:7). Heaven is the eternal home of Christians (2 Cor. 5:1–2). Ephesians 2:6 reminds us that, even now, we are seated with Christ in heaven (part of the eternal promise made to Christ-followers and sealed by the Holy Spirit).

Paul's Thorn in the Flesh (12:7–8)

Paul countered any form of boasting by immediately mentioning his "thorn in the flesh." Although not specified, the thorn was likely one of three things:

1. It could have been the opposition that he had faced wherever he went, which included the Jews who did not want the Christian faith to grow. Initially, Paul was one of the champions of the anti-Christian faction within the Jewish community before he became one of the church's early leaders. There would have indeed been Jewish opposition. As is evident within this letter, Paul also had significant resistance within the early church itself. Christian leaders, vying for control, besmirched Paul and his reputation. Finally, there was hostility from civic leaders along Paul's journey, as well from the Roman Empire in general, with the goal of keeping the peace.

2. Paul's thorn in the flesh could have been a physical disorder. Paul listed the physical sufferings he had to endure because of his apostleship: prison, floggings, beatings, stoning, various dangers, hunger, and such (2 Cor. 11:23–28). Undoubtedly, these would have inflicted severe physical trauma. He had to have experienced broken bones, torn skin, lacerated muscles, and injury to internal organs. Some of these may have healed; others may have not. Any of them could have been a "thorn" in his body. However, it was his illness

that led him to begin his ministry to the Galatians (Gal. 4:13–14).

Galatians 5:11 also hints that Paul may have had poor vision: "See what large letters I use as I write to you with my own hand." Perhaps Paul had trouble writing altogether, which would make sense given the beatings and stoning he endured. Natural ailments such as arthritis, are also plausible. Paul used other people to write his letters (see Rom. 16:22); he only penned a line or two as evidence of his authorship (1 Cor. 16:21; Col. 4:18; 2 Thess. 3:17).

3. Paul's thorn in the flesh could have been a relational or emotional issue stemming from time away from his family or absences from the multiple churches he served. Absence can drive a wedge between those separated. The relationships Paul had built at previous churches or while on missionary trips were interrupted continuously for the next opportunity. Those movements would have taken an emotional toll on his relationships, such as when the Ephesian leaders wept, embraced him, kissed him, and grieved thinking "they would never see his face again." (Acts 20:36–38).

Like anyone else, Paul would have had good and bad days—filled with anger, frustration, disappointment, sadness, and perhaps depression. He was in spiritual warfare always. Although he learned to be content (1 Timothy 6:6) and live at peace (Phil. 4:7, 9), such spiritual battles were exhausting.

We deal with these same three issues. We may face opposition in our families, neighborhoods, workplaces, communities, and even in our churches. We cannot let that opposition impede us from being who we need to be for the sake of Christ. We also deal with many different physical, relational, and emotional issues over the course of a lifetime. Following Jesus does not make us immune from problems. Paul had his thorn, and we have ours. To deal with it we must embrace the same grace in Christ that Paul held close.

Paul referred to the thorn as a "messenger of Satan," but that God allowed it by not removing it. How can something be from Satan and God at the same time? Because God is in ultimate control, Satan tries his best to affect our lives adversely, but God can and does mean all for good. Prime examples are the cross of Jesus, and when the sons of Jacob sold their brother Joseph into slavery. Joseph later responded, "You intended to harm me, but God intended it for good" (Genesis 50:20). Paul wrote in Romans 8:28, "And we know that in all things God works for the good of those who love him, who have been called according to his purpose."

It is also important to note that we all go through things we would prefer to avoid. God does not always provide immediate deliverance, but that does not mean he doesn't care. He loves us and is continually working for our good.

Paul Experienced God's Sufficient Grace (12:9–10)

Jesus' reply to our thorns is, "My grace is sufficient for you." This response has three important parts.

1. The grace is sufficient to cover all issues in life, whatever thorns that may dig in. The word "sufficient" is the translation of the Greek word *arkei,* which means *enough, satisfying, full, content, nothing left wanting.* It is the feeling after a large holiday meal when those who feasted cannot eat another crumb. It is the feeling of not needing anything and having a satisfied, bliss-filled moment. This kind of sufficient grace is the anesthetic remedy for any thorn in the flesh.

2. The grace is from Jesus. He claimed it as "My grace." Jesus has given us many gifts: salvation, care, provision, guidance, reconciliation, friendship, power to overcome, etc., and his grace is an extension of these.

3. His grace is for you. It is personal. It is not a general response to the whole world. It is personal and intimate as each person is in need. For each potential thorn, imagine Jesus saying, "My grace is sufficient for *you.*"

Paul also said that his human weakness was the canvas on which God demonstrated his divine power and strength. Power is made perfect in weakness. Where personal weakness exists, strength also lives. The formula Paul wrote is this: our weakness plus Jesus' strength equals godly power.

Implications and Actions

God has promised grace to meet our needs. Like Paul, we can find comfort from the Lord in whatever thorns we may have. Like Paul, we must lean into the strength and power Jesus provides through his grace. We cannot boast of our abilities and strengths. Such pride will ultimately prove our downfall. Instead, we must walk in humility and trust in the thoroughly satisfying grace of Jesus. We must acknowledge our frailties but not live in them. We must not allow our thorns to undo us, but overcome them through the power of God.

Third Heaven

Paul used the term "third heaven" to refer to where he met God during one experience, and possibly four other incidents as well. What exactly is the third heaven? The term *first heaven* was used by the ancient Hebrews to refer to the sky and atmosphere. It is where birds flew, clouds floated, mountains rose, and trees grew. The Hebrews defined the *second heaven* as the abode of the sun, moon, and stars. Today, we would call this outer sphere "space." The ancient writers described the *third heaven* as the abode of God. It was beyond the first two heavens and would signify the spiritual realm. Paul expressed ambiguity and uncertainty about his experience, unsure if he was taken in body or spirit. He also used the term *paradise*, which may be synonymous with heaven or perhaps Paul meant an additional dominion as well.

Sufficient Grace in Weakness

We have all felt ill-prepared for tasks which may demonstrate our inexperience, uncertainty, inability, or fears. How have you experienced sufficient grace in the face of the following:

- Surrendering your life to Jesus
- Getting married
- First day on a job
- Taking your first baby home
- In a church dealing with problems
- After the death of a loved one

Questions

1. Describe a tough time when you were comforted by experiencing the presence of God.

2. How have your personal thorns been paralyzing, frustrating, or shut you down from being who you were called to be?

3. Can you relate to Paul's plea of removing his "thorn?" Describe a time when you had to forge through something you did not want to experience.

4. How have you experienced the sufficient grace of God?

5. How have you experienced power in weakness?

Our Next New Study

(Available for use beginning December 2018)

Grace and Truth

A STUDY OF THE GOSPEL OF JOHN

HOW TO ORDER
More Bible Study Materials

It's easy! Just fill in the following information. For additional Bible study materials available in print or digital formats see www.baptistwaypress.org, or get a catalog of available print materials by calling 1-866-249-1799 or e-mailing baptistway@texasbaptists.org.

Title of item	Price	Quantity	Cost
This Issue			
Correction and Counsel (1 & 2 Corinthians)—Study Guide (BWP001262)	$4.50	_____	_____
Correction and Counsel (1 & 2 Corinthians)—Large Print Study Guide (BWP001263)	$4.75	_____	_____
Correction and Counsel (1 & 2 Corinthians)—Teaching Guide (BWP001264)	$5.25	_____	_____
Additional Issues Available:			
Thematic Studies			
Rescue and Redemption—Study Guide (BWP001257)	$4.50	_____	_____
Rescue and Redemption—Large Print Study Guide (BWP001258)	$4.75	_____	_____
Rescue and Redemption—Teaching Guide (BWP001259)	$5.25	_____	_____
Called to Serve—Study Guide (BWP001237)	$4.50	_____	_____
Called to Serve—Large Print Study Guide (BWP001238)	$4.75	_____	_____
Called to Serve—Teaching Guide (BWP001239)	$5.25	_____	_____
Faith > Fear—Study Guide (BWP001217)	$4.50	_____	_____
Faith > Fear—Large Print Study Guide (BWP001218)	$4.75	_____	_____
Faith > Fear—Teaching Guide (BWP001219)	$5.25	_____	_____
Created for Relationships—Study Guide (BWP001197)	$4.50	_____	_____
Created for Relationships—Large Print Study Guide (BWP001198)	$4.75	_____	_____
Created for Relationships—Teaching Guide (BWP001199)	$5.25	_____	_____
Old Testament			
Power & Purpose: God Unveils the Universe (Genesis 1-11)—Study Guide (BWP001232)	$4.50	_____	_____
Power & Purpose: God Unveils the Universe (Genesis 1-11)—Large Print Study Guide (BWP001233)	$4.75	_____	_____
Power & Purpose: God Unveils the Universe (Genesis 1-11)—Teaching Guide (BWP001234)	$5.25	_____	_____
Exodus: Liberated for Life in Covenant with God—Study Guide (BWP001192)	$4.50	_____	_____
Exodus: Liberated for Life in Covenant with God—Large Print Study Guide (BWP001193)	$4.75	_____	_____
Exodus: Liberated for Life in Covenant with God—Teaching Guide (BWP001194)	$5.25	_____	_____
Choices and Consequences (Joshua/Judges)—Study Guide (BWP001212)	$4.50	_____	_____
Choices and Consequences (Joshua/Judges)—Large Print Study Guide (BWP001213)	$4.75	_____	_____
Choices and Consequences (Joshua/Judges)—Teaching Guide (BWP001214)	$5.25	_____	_____
Character and the Crown (1 Samuel)—Study Guide (BWP001252)	$4.50	_____	_____
Character and the Crown (1 Samuel)—Large Print Study Guide (BWP001253)	$4.75	_____	_____
Character and the Crown (1 Samuel)—Teaching Guide (BWP001254)	$5.25	_____	_____
New Testament			
Jesus: King or Concierge? (Matthew)—Study Guide (BWP001207)	$4.50	_____	_____
Jesus: King or Concierge? (Matthew)—Large Print Study Guide (BWP001208)	$4.75	_____	_____
Jesus: King or Concierge? (Matthew)—Teaching Guide (BWP001209)	$5.25	_____	_____
On Your Mark: The Gospel in Motion (Mark)—Study Guide (BWP001227)	$4.50	_____	_____
On Your Mark: The Gospel in Motion (Mark)—Large Print Study Guide (BWP001228)	$4.75	_____	_____
On Your Mark: The Gospel in Motion (Mark)—Teaching Guide (BWP001229)	$5.25	_____	_____
GSI: Gospel Story Investigator (Luke)—Study Guide (BWP001247)	$4.50	_____	_____
GSI: Gospel Story Investigator (Luke)—Large Print Study Guide (BWP001248)	$4.75	_____	_____
GSI: Gospel Story Investigator (Luke)—Teaching Guide (BWP001249)	$5.25	_____	_____
Going Viral: The Birth and Advance of the Church (Acts)—Study Guide (BWP001242)	$4.50	_____	_____
Going Viral: The Birth and Advance of the Church (Acts)—Large Print Study Guide (BWP001243)	$4.75	_____	_____
Going Viral: The Birth and Advance of the Church (Acts)—Teaching Guide (BWP001244)	$5.25	_____	_____

Romans: A Gospel-Centered Worldview—Study Guide (BWP001202) $4.50   _____   _____

Romans: A Gospel-Centered Worldview—Large Print Study Guide (BWP001203) $4.75   _____   _____

Romans: A Gospel-Centered Worldview—Teaching Guide (BWP001204) $5.25   _____   _____

Terror & Triumph (Revelation)—Study Guide (BWP001222) $4.50   _____   _____

Terror & Triumph (Revelation)—Large Print Study Guide (BWP001223) $4.75   _____   _____

Terror & Triumph (Revelation)—Teaching Guide (BWP001224) $5.25   _____   _____

Coming for use beginning December 2018

Grace and Truth (John) —Study Guide (BWP001267) $4.50   _____   _____

Grace and Truth (John) —Large Print Study Guide (BWP001268) $4.75   _____   _____

Grace and Truth (John) —Teaching Guide (BWP001269) $5.25   _____   _____

━━━ PLEASE NOTE ━━━

In addition to these Bible studies, which are available in both print and digital formats, we have several studies available in a digital-only format. See www.baptistwaypress.org for a complete listing of these studies.

Standard (UPS/Mail) Shipping Charges*			
Order Value	Shipping charge**	Order Value	Shipping charge**
$.01–$9.99	$6.50	$160.00–$199.99	$24.00
$10.00–$19.99	$8.50	$200.00–$249.99	$28.00
$20.00–$39.99	$9.50	$250.00–$299.99	$30.00
$40.00–$59.99	$10.50	$300.00–$349.99	$34.00
$60.00–$79.99	$11.50	$350.00–$399.99	$42.00
$80.00–$99.99	$12.50	$400.00–$499.99	$50.00
$100.00–$129.99	$15.00	$500.00–$599.99	$60.00
$130.00–$159.99	$20.00	$600.00–$799.99	$72.00**

Cost of items (Order value)   _____

Shipping charges (see chart*)   _____

TOTAL   _____

*Please call 1-866-249-1799 if the exact amount is needed prior to ordering.

**For order values $800.00 and above, please call 1-866-249-1799 or check www.baptistwaypress.org

Please allow three weeks for standard delivery. For express shipping service: Call 1-866-249-1799 for information on additional charges.

YOUR NAME _____   PHONE _____

YOUR CHURCH _____   DATE ORDERED _____

STREET ADDRESS _____

CITY _____   STATE _____   ZIP CODE _____

E-MAIL _____

MAIL this form with your check for the total amount to:
BAPTISTWAY PRESS, Baptist General Convention of Texas,
7557 Rambler Road, Suite 1200, Dallas, TX 75231–2388
(Make checks to "BaptistWay Press")

OR, **CALL** your order toll-free: 1-866-249-1799
(M-Fri 8:30 a.m.-5:00 p.m. central time).

OR, **E-MAIL** your order to: baptistway@texasbaptists.org.

OR, **ORDER ONLINE** at www.baptistwaypress.org.

We look forward to receiving your order! Thank you!